The People's H

Old Murders and Crimes of Northumberland and Tyne & Wear

by

Paul Heslop

For my family

First published in 2002 by

The People's History Ltd
Suite 1
Byron House
Seaham Grange Business Park
Seaham
Co. Durham
SR7 0PY

ISBN 1 902527 65 8

Contents

Foreword
by Arthur McKenzie

Nothing fascinates us more than a grisly, chilling or bizarre murder. The subject revolts, yet draws us in and no more so than crimes from the dim and distant past. The images conjured seem to be in black and white and shrouded in mystery without the benefit of CCTV, forensic scientists and DNA. In those sepia days it was down to simple police work, sheer luck, or a hapless person was seen or associated with the victim and immediately nominated for the crime by police and a public eager for retribution.

In many cases the perpetrator was caught in the twinkling of an eye, and before you could blink he or she was hung with alarming speed. Justice done and never denied, or so the public thought; but Paul Heslop questions whether this was expedience or blatant injustice. A detective himself for over twenty years, Paul knows the inner workings of the intricate machinery that drives the world of cops and criminals. In his book *Old Murders and Crimes of Northumberland and Tyne & Wear* he goes back to retrace and examine several of our heinous crimes, some well documented, others more shadowy.

Paul not only investigates in great detail, but visits scenes, unearths public records and digs into the nitty-gritty as he looks for evidence upon which the offenders could be prosecuted to conviction in today's climate. He doesn't shrink in his evaluation. His conclusions include blatant police 'fit ups', political corruption and downright incompetence. He questions whether the right person was convicted, and persuasively argues that many who swung from the hangman's rope were, if not innocent, at least deserving the benefit of the doubt. In strong, personal terms he deals with the subject of hanging, setting out its history, documenting blunders that occurred in the name of justice. With his forensic eye and a strong sense of humour Paul brings the weight of his experience and masterful gift of research to this book which will prove absorbing reading for anyone interested in the law and true crimes.

Introduction

The 'old murders and crimes' which appear in this book were perpetrated in what, since 1974, is the area covered by Northumbria Police: the county of Northumberland and the Metropolitan County of Tyne and Wear, formed by the cities of Newcastle upon Tyne and Sunderland, and the boroughs of North Tyneside, South Tyneside and Gateshead (except two: the murder of Caroline Winter at Seaham, in County Durham, and the murder of Sydney Dunn, the Newcastle taxi driver, who may or may not have been killed also in County Durham, but I would not propose to be so pedantic that material I consider relevant should be omitted from these pages).

'Northumbria', insofar as the police area of that name is concerned, is a misnomer anyway. Northumbria once covered an area north of the Humber (north-humber-land) to the Firth of Forth, and later was an acceptable name for northern England, from, say, York to the England-Scotland border. One supposes, since the police area excluded County Durham and North Yorkshire, that 'Northumbria Police' was a name of convenience, to be preferred to 'Northumberland and Tyne and Wear Police'. Confusing, perhaps, but I am loth to say 'old murders and crimes in Northumbria' when this is incorrect.

Detective Sergeant Paul Heslop (extreme left, middle row) at the Metropolitan Police Training School, Hendon.

'Truth will come to light; murder cannot be hid long.'

William Shakespeare
(from *The Merchant of Venice*)

Physically and intellectually, Thomas Fury was far above the ordinary class of criminal. It is a matter of wonder that a man of his mental capacity should be a criminal when he qualified by his intelligence and extensive reading to be so much better.

The brutality of the crime he committed is evidence of how deeply engrafted in him were the debasing influences of his childhood. In a moment of frenzy, and mad with drink and passion at the thought of being robbed, he cruelly stabbed his victim through the heart no less than ten times, inflicting wounds of a frightful character.

He never once exhibited the slightest fear at his approaching death, chiefly occupying his mornings and evenings in writing and reading, and every day he enjoyed a good sleep after dinner.

There was not the semblance of flinching or fear in his countenance as he placed himself underneath the fatal noose. Then Marwood stepped back, raised the lever and in an instant the false door gave way and Thomas Fury fell with a heavy thud. A momentary quivering of his body and all was over. His neck was broken. Death was instantaneous, and the black flag was run up the flagstaff over the prison gateway.

Sunderland Daily Echo, 17th May, 1882.

A STARK REMINDER

Winter's Gibbet today, Steng Cross, on the lonely
Northumberland moors.

It's a bleak, windswept place, where the Northumbrian moors reach to far horizons, a land of green rolling hills, with deep, unseen valleys and distant forests. Steng Cross marks the highest point of the old drove road, a place unchanged for centuries, except that today, on approach, one's eyes are drawn to the tall gibbet standing stark and unexpectedly on the skyline and nearing, the gruesome wooden head, swinging eerily in the wind.

Scots once drove their cattle to English markets this way, and travellers came on horseback and by coach. It was for their benefit that, in 1792, the corpse of convicted murderer William Winter was hung here, and left to rot until his bones sank into the earth; and after, to be replaced by a wooden effigy and now, over 200 years on, a wooden head with unseeing eyes, facing the spot where he allegedly murdered an old woman in her humble home.

Today, few people occupy the southern hinterlands of the Cheviots; but it wasn't always so. In the 18th century there were large farming communities and coal workings in the area, and two miles to the north of Elsdon, in the tiny hamlet of Raw, old Margaret Crozier lived in a pele tower, a left-over edifice from the days when families lived in fear of invading Scots and Reivers. The pele also served as her drapery shop. Locals and passers-by came this way to avoid the turnpike road over Steng Cross, but it was two local women, Bessie Jackson, a farmer's daughter, and Mary Temple, a 'needlewoman', who spent sociable time with Margaret during the evening of Monday, 29th August, 1791, chatting at the door.

Raw Pele today: a farm building, the haunt of hungry chickens.

The sound of dogs barking seemed to cause concern to Margaret's visitors, who warned of the possible presence of strangers. 'Make sure you bolt your door tonight,' said Bessie, as she and Mary left. Margaret did indeed bolt her door, but it did no good. That night, someone forced the oak bolt aside, and the following morning she was found dead in her bed with her throat cut.

It was another neighbour, Barbara Drummond, who suspected something was amiss when she came to call. She noticed thread lying outside and told William Dodds, a joiner, who went upstairs and found Margaret. Yet the wound to her throat was not deep, certainly not fatal; a handkerchief was tied around her mouth, possibly to keep her from screaming, so it seems she died from suffocation. The palms of her hands were cut, tell-tale signs that she had tried to defend herself against someone with a knife, and one was found, a 'gully', or meat knife, among her bedclothes. It had an iron hoop around the shaft where it connected with the blade. Outside, in the soil, were found distinctive footprint patterns, consistent with nailed boots. The circumstances in which Margaret Crozier was found lends doubt as to who killed her, as events would show.

Word soon spread, and two boys reported seeing strangers the day before Margaret was killed. One of them, 11-year old Robert Hindmarsh of Whiskershiel, gave a clear account of what he had seen. There had been three strangers – a man and two women – by a sheepfold near Whitlees Farm, only three miles from Raw. They had been eating mutton, which the man carved with a large 'gully'; Robert recalled it had an iron hoop around the shaft. He also noticed the nails in the man's shoes, as he lay on the grass.

Descriptions of these persons were given. The man was six feet tall, powerfully built, with a dark complexion and long dark hair, gathered or 'clubbed' behind his head. He wore a light-coloured coat, light blue breeches and grey stockings. The women were tall, of stout build, wearing grey cloaks and bonnets – common garb for those times. One of them, the younger, wore a light-coloured cotton gown beneath her cloak.

Three parish constables set off on horseback in pursuit. The direction they took, south, may have been somewhat fortuitous, although there were reports of three people with an ass seen near Harlow Hill, in Roman Wall country. They came upon a gang of men mending the road near Horsley, twenty miles away, who reported that a man with 'clubbed hair' had passed by shortly before and indicated the direction he had taken. On horseback, the three lawmen soon caught up and arrested William Winter. He gave them no trouble.

Soon after, a young woman in a cotton gown was detained at Ovingham. She was brought face to face with Winter, and each denied knowing the other. But she had a dog, which clearly knew the man, and soon after she admitted she and Winter were acquainted. She was Jane Clark of Hedley Hall, near Ryton. It wasn't long before the other woman, Eleanor Clark, possibly identified by Jane, her sister, was arrested. And when the soles of the boots worn by Winter were compared with the marks found outside Margaret Crozier's home, it seemed they were a perfect match.

The three were said to be members of a 'Faw' gang, or gypsies, renowned for stealing. They were taken before a magistrate, Mr Mitford. William Winter's shirt was bloodstained which, he explained, was down to fighting. But the magistrate rejected this, saying it was to his knowledge that gypsies fought bare-chested! They were sent to Morpeth gaol to await trial at the County Assizes, in those days held once a year. Meanwhile, it seems the women's mother, also known as Jane Clark, or Gregg, was arrested a few days after. Evidently she taught members of her family to steal and it was said she had been seen hanging around Raw pele earlier, so maybe she set the crime up, as they say.

A year later, Winter, Jane and Eleanor Clark stood trial at the Moot Hall, Newcastle, charged with the murder of Margaret Crozier. A 'great crowd' was present to hear the two boys give their evidence of identification, although what the procedure was in 'identifying' any of the prisoners, either at the time of their arrest or later, isn't known.

Old Castle Keep, Newcastle. William Winter and his two women accomplices were incarcerated here in 1792.

Even so, young Robert Hindmarsh's testimony about the 'gully knife' and Winter's shoes must have carried much weight. And when Elizabeth Jackson, Margaret Crozier's neighbour, identified a night-cap and apron, found in possession of Jane Clark, as the very items she had given to the deceased, the game was up. The mother, Jane Clark senior, was released. One can only assume there was no evidence to support the story that she had 'set up' the crime, or perhaps the prosecution in those days focused on the murder only, and the grim events that would follow.

William Winter admitted breaking into Margaret Crozier's home, and even cutting her throat, but said he had left her alive – and it was true that the wound to her throat was not a fatal one. He said he sent the women 'back' to tie her up to prevent her calling for help. If so, the two women, Jane and Eleanor, were also in Margaret's home – but was it they, and not William Winter, who murdered her? Or was Winter merely trying to shift blame? Both women denied taking any part in the crime, and sobbed throughout their trial. The evidence, as far as the murder goes, seems inconclusive. But maybe I write from a different perspective, born of experience in a world over 200 years after this crime. Perhaps in the late eighteenth century common criminals were all regarded as guilty as each other, and never mind who did what. They were gypsies, Margaret Crozier had been murdered and they had been caught. The rules of justice, such as they were, did not favour their class so they were all condemned.

William Winter was a strong man, mentally and physically. Throughout the trial he showed no emotion, certainly not fear, and even told the balding judge he was in need of his wig! When Jane Clark, distraught, fainted in the dock at the 'guilty' verdict, Winter, despite being shackled in heavy irons, picked her up and carried her out. As he left the court, someone, possibly one of his 'Faw' friends, offered him a half-gallon of ale, which he drank cheerfully before proceeding with the women to the castle gaol.

On 10th August 1792 William Winter, and Jane and Eleanor Clark were placed upon a cart and taken to Newgate Prison, Newcastle, where they were hanged, the sobbing women still protesting their innocence. In keeping with practice of the time the women's bodies were sent for dissection in the name of medical science. Winter's body, instead of being buried, was taken back to the lonely Northumbrian moors, to Steng Cross, where it was hung from a thirty-foot high gibbet in sight of the scene of his crime and still clad in the clothes he wore, and bound in strips of steel, for passers-by to see as a warning to those who would contemplate murder.

And there Winter's corpse remained, for months thereafter until, decaying and rotting, the clothing fell away and the flesh fell from his bones. Finally, when the bones began to fall they were buried, but to perpetuate the message the authorities erected a wooden replica corpse which hung from the gibbet until it, too, rotted, and in the 1850s was replaced by a carved, wooden head. What a sight it must have been for

Elsdon.

those who passed this way: but was it a gruesome warning to those who would murder, or testimony to a ghastly miscarriage of justice?

The pele at Raw still stands, now incorporated into farm buildings housing cattle and visited by hungry chickens. A replica stands on the spot of the old gibbet, of which nothing of the original remains. Today's wooden head, swinging and creaking thirty feet above the ground, is no longer there to deter would-be murderers with the stark message of 'this could be you'; rather, to some extent, it serves the cause of tourism. You can see it in today's colourful brochures. Would that Margaret Crozier could have known her death had not been altogether in vain!

Evistones. The Rustlers' village lies beneath the ground on a landscape now the domain of Cheviot sheep.

Point to Ponder

Why did we execute people? As a punishment? As fitting retribution for their crimes – an eye for an eye? As a deterrent to others who would kill?

Let the punishment fit the crime, for a start. Hanging people, as we did, for such 'crimes' as being in the company of gypsies for a month and cases where children aged 7-14 years showed evidence of 'malice' was hardly fair; rather they were crimes against those higher up the social scale than society as a whole. Hanging people for murder was 'fitting retribution', but that doesn't mean it was right. A deterrent? Many, perhaps most, murders are 'domestic', where offender and victim are known to one another; they are often committed by men who are drunk, hardly the sort who might stop and consider 'if I do this they will hang me'. He's drunk, he's lost it, he kills. He never got out of bed that morning to do it; it happened. Gibbeting William Winter and others like him might have prevented others from killing, but it is doubtful. There is no way of knowing how many thought about the consequences and did or didn't commit murder thereafter.

The ruined tower, all that remains above ground at Evistones.

13

The Rustlers' Village

Up to the end of the 16th century, crime along the border country of England and Scotland was a byword. This was the 'debateable land', the domain of the so-called Border Reivers who rode at night to steal and rustle cattle. They came from every rung of the social strata, from gentleman and peer to smallholder and labourer. It is no wonder today's maps are punctuated with castles, fortified farmhouses (bastles) and ruined pele towers, solid stone edifices with walls several feet thick. The latter served as sanctuary for peaceful folk, and often fleeing raiders, pursued 'hot trod' over the moors by furious owners of rustled cattle or rival gangs.

In Redesdale, near the border, are the remains of Evistones, a deserted moorland village. Here, sunken stones and an abandoned tower are testimony to its long-gone inhabitants whose one thing in common was that they were thieves. They had to be, for the folk of Redesdale were shunned by fellow Northumbrians, barred from making an honest buck, so that the only alternative to feed starving families was to steal. 'When the larder is bare the only way to fill it is by emptying someone else's', and they did. A far cry from today – stealing cars, mobile phones and other gadgetry for greed or to finance drugs – the night-riders of Evistones stole to live.

Today, the old tower stands defiantly on the windswept hillside, its vaulted roof covered by grass, its only visitors the sheep who wander among the boulders and mounds of a long-abandoned community. The men no longer ride at night on their unlawful missions; their wives no longer prepare meals, not knowing if they will return. Only their ghosts remain, unseen spirits who may yet dwell in the lost village of Evistones.

Elsdon Tower. A medieval towerhouse, 'one of the best preserved buildings in Notthumberland', it occupied a naturally defensive position, providing refuge from Scottish raiders and Reivers.

A WICKED CONSPIRACY

Church of St John the Baptist, Edlingham.

A cold chisel, two pieces of torn newspaper, a series of footprint impressions. This was the evidence, according to the police, that proved two local men, labourers Peter Murphy, 22, and Michael Brannagan, 44, committed burglary and wounded the Reverend Matthew Buckle and his daughter Georgina at the vicarage in 19th century Edlingham, near Alnwick. A sleepy place, Edlingham nestles in a deep valley, surrounded by rugged Northumbrian countryside where little has changed: the church still stands proud and silent, the former vicarage just up the hill, nearby a ruined castle and scattered houses in grey Northumbrian stone.

Today, a notice in the church says the Reverend Buckle was vicar in 1839 and thereafter for 52 years. He could not have foreseen that, forty years after his appointment, events would take place on the night of 7-8th February, 1879 when, but for the grace of God, he and his daughter would have been murdered by armed men who broke into the vicarage. Nor blamed for his mistaken belief in the 'energy, promptitude and intelligence' of the police, whom he thus described in a letter to a local newspaper; and he would not have condoned the imprisonment of two men, falsely accused and wrongly convicted of the burglary, thanks to the wicked conspiracy of those very policemen who, in modern-day language, fitted them up.

Edlingham vicarage.

Imagine, if you will, the scene on that dark February night, as Mr Buckle, 77, his invalid wife, daughter Georgina and four women servants slept soundly in the old vicarage. It was Georgina who heard the noise, around one in the morning, and in those Victorian days, with no telephone to summon assistance, she woke her father with the news that they had burglars. If the old man had gathered his family around him and let the intruders take what they could, who could have blamed him? Instead, he lit a candle, put on his dressing gown, picked up the sword he kept by his bed for such emergencies and followed by plucky Georgina ventured downstairs – she having refused his bidding to lock herself in her mother's room.

Two men had forced their way into the drawing room, one armed with an iron bar or a gun, Mr Buckle could not be certain in the flickering candlelight. As his candle went out, and brandishing his sword, Mr Buckle 'went at' the man who carried the firearm, as it was, for the intruder fired a shot. Mr Buckle was hit on the shoulder by pellets and splintered wood from the nearby door frame. In his letter to the *Alnwick Mercury*, he said: 'I ran my sword three or four inches into his body'. The man did not fall, and Mr Buckle felt the blade might have merely penetrated his clothing. He kept him at sword point until he heard the intruder ramming a second charge into his gun, at which point Georgina dragged her father out of the way and the men escaped. Only then did Mr Buckle realise his daughter had also suffered injury. The burglars' visit was not in vain; they fled with Georgina's gold watch.

Mr Buckle wrote: 'No daughter could have shown more heroic devotion in seeking to protect her father's life at the price of her own'. It was 'not until she had bathed his wounds, called the servants, roused the village and dispatched a man on horseback for medical assistance and the police that she acknowledged herself wounded dangerously'. Fortunately, neither he nor his daughter was badly hurt. The police arrived with commendable speed. Sad to say, it is the only commendable thing to be said of the police in this case, although it would be years before the truth of their wicked conspiracy came out. For now it seemed their actions were quite brilliant.

The officer in charge was Superintendent Harkes, who wasted no time in searching for clues and sending officers to visit the homes of known poachers and other likely lads. He examined the window through which the burglars had entered and departed, and discovered the marks of their feet and knees in the soft earth. He was handed a chisel and a piece of torn newspaper, the latter discovered outside the dining room door where the struggle with Mr Buckle had occurred.

Murphy and Brannagan, renowned poachers, were stopped on the road by police and taken in as suspects. Neither was armed. At 7 a.m. they were allowed to go home – whereupon the police turned up to search for evidence. Brannagan was still removing his dirty clogs when they arrived and arrested him again. They seized Murphy's boots and Brannagan's clogs. Each had certain characteristics, the police would

Moot Hall, Newcastle upon Tyne – venue of the Assize Court, today the Crown Court.

say, which matched them to the impressions in the earth outside the dining room window. John Redpath, Murphy's brother-in-law, was shown the chisel, which he identified as his. It appeared it had been used to force the window and the drawing room door and was linked to Murphy at least.

Neither suspect had any injuries that may have been inflicted by a sword. Nor was their clothing cut, as might have been expected. Both men were taken to the vicarage where Mr Buckle and Georgina failed to identify them, hardly surprising as events had occurred in near total darkness. Police officers and members of the legal profession will shudder at a procedure contrary to today's identification laws, where suspects appear on identification parades under strict rules.

The police had wasted no time in apprehending those they believed to be the culprits and securing most of the 'evidence' that would lead to their conviction. But this would prove to be a classic case of over-zealous police who, believing they had arrested the right men, sought for and provided 'evidence' to support what they believed, instead of seeking out the truth without pre-judged opinion. Peter Murphy and Michael Brannagan would lose their liberty for seven years as a result. It might have been worse; had Mr Buckle or his daughter died that night, they would surely have swung.

Murphy and Brannagan appeared at the Newcastle Assizes in April, 1879, before Justice Manisty. They were charged with stealing Georgina Buckle's gold watch and chain and seal, and unlawfully and feloniously shooting 'with a gun loaded with leaden shot' with intent to murder, and inflicting bodily injury to the Buckles. They pleaded not guilty. The judge's father, coincidentally, was vicar at Edlingham immediately before the Rev Buckle.

Mr Buckle said he believed the weapon in the hands of one of the intruders to be an iron bar, not a gun. It was his opinion that burglars seldom carried guns. For this reason he prodded his assailant rather than running him through with the sword as he could have. He believed he might have pierced the skin, certainly the man's clothing. An hour later the cook, Jane Brown, handed him the chisel. It seemed the window and drawing room door had been forced with it. Although the candle had gone out, Georgina caught a glimpse of the other man in the moonlight through the window. She did not see the man who fired the gun.

William Sanderson, farm manager at Edlingham, said that early next morning he searched the outhouse and discovered two impressions in the hay. The intruders had evidently spent time there before breaking into the vicarage. He went into the dining room where he found a piece of newspaper, which he handed to Supt Harkes. Sanderson was asked if a piece of paper he was shown was the same one he had found. He said he took it to be.

Dr Wilson had examined the prisoners at Alnwick police station, finding neither prisoner's skin broken. Either Mr Buckle was incorrect in thinking he had penetrated his assailant's skin; or, if he did stab one of the intruders, the police had made at least one wrong arrest. Dr Wilson said that on 16th February, over a week after the burglary, he had examined the pockets of Murphy's coat, finding a piece of newspaper between the lining and one of the pockets. The police said this matched exactly the piece of newspaper found in the vicarage. Supt Harkes said the drawing room window had been forced from outside. The drawing room door had also been forced. After being handed the chisel he compared it to the marks made at each location and found it fitted exactly. Outside, next to the window, he saw two sets of footprints which led through the grounds to the road.

The prisoners' clothing had been taken by Inspector Harrison and handed to Supt Harkes. The inspector took the prisoners' boots and clogs to the scene, finding they corresponded to the footprints in the earth. He took plaster casts of the impressions, which he now produced. He was asked why he had not discovered the piece of newspaper in Murphy's jacket – found over a week later by Dr Wilson. He said he had failed to find it. Sergeant Gare said that nearly a month after the burglary he found a piece of corduroy and a button outside the drawing room window. The corduroy fitted into a place in Brannagan's trousers where a piece was missing. Asked why it had not been found earlier, Sgt Gare said snow had fallen and covered it. The judge refused to allow the jury to hear this testimony, saying it was 'too dangerous to put weight on it'. Why? Didn't he believe him?

John Redpath, a crucial witness as far as the chisel was concerned, was too ill to give evidence. Agnes Simm, Murphy's girlfriend, said Redpath was short-sighted, and had not been allowed to hold the chisel in his hand when shown it by the police. Redpath was 'a blind old man', whose reply, when asked by police if the chisel taken from the pantry was his said 'if it was found in the pantry it must be'. Some identification!

No gun was found. Otherwise, the prosecution evidence seemed damning – the 'identification' of the chisel, the matching pieces of torn newspaper (and the evidence of the piece of corduroy, not heard by the jury), and feet impressions found at the scene. There was no evidence of identification, and no admissions. It took the jury three hours to return 'guilty' verdicts on two men whose only previous convictions were for poaching, none for violence or stealing. They were guilty of the 'gravest offences', said the judge. Had Georgina Buckle not restrained her father they would surely have committed murder. It was a miracle they were not being condemned to death. He sentenced them to life imprisonment.

The judge praised the police for their thoroughness and 'swift apprehension of the culprits'. He was right on the former point, for Supt Harkes had been very thorough indeed, and utterly wrong on the second, for the men responsible for this crime were still at large. Meanwhile, Murphy and Brannagan began their long prison sentences, 'life' then meaning twenty years minimum. They protested their innocence in letters to their families. One can barely imagine the feelings of Murphy, who ended up in Portsmouth, and Brannagan who was sent to Dartmoor. There was nothing more to be done: no DNA, blood grouping and fingerprint evidence existed then to eliminate them from the crime. Their case seemed hopeless.

But rumours abounded. Everyone knew they were poachers, but neither was known to carry a gun. They had used a terrier to catch rabbits. Burglary was not their style. Then an Alnwick solicitor, hearing that another local poacher, George Edgell, had been out on the night in question, told the Rev Jevon Perry, an Alnwick vicar, who confronted Edgell about it. Told the vicar, not the police. A sad indictment of the local force. Edgell confessed. He said he and another local criminal, Charles Richardson, had committed the crime. Richardson, said Edgell, had fired the gun. Criminals who play a lesser part in committing crime are prone to spill the beans on accomplices whose activities are more serious.

Edgell confirmed they had used a chisel to force entry into the vicarage. They'd found it in an outhouse on the vicarage premises. It belonged to the Rev Buckle! Richardson, he said, had taken Georgina's gold watch and chain, which had long been disposed of. The watch, or a trinket attached to it, he'd sold to a jeweller in Newcastle who confirmed Edgell's account. Edgell said he and Richardson had worn sacking over their feet when they committed the burglary, hardly in keeping with the 'footprints' discovered by the police, and the plaster impressions so painstakingly taken to prove they matched the boots and clogs of Murphy and Brannagan.

The piece of newspaper 'found' in Murphy's jacket was planted evidence. It is probable that the police somehow persuaded Dr Wilson to examine the coat, for wouldn't it look better if such damning evidence was found by a doctor instead of a policeman?

Edgell and Richardson stood trial before a different judge, Mr Baron Pollock. Edgell admitted his part, and the evidence against Richardson, including testimony from Edgell against his accomplice, led to their convictions. Richardson's gun was, perhaps, the same one used to murder Police Constable George Grey at Eglingham, 6 years before, for which he, Richardson, had been acquitted. One might wonder why the police didn't bring him in on suspicion of the Edlingham job. Clearly their minds were made up. Incredibly, the police response was that the officers had merely been over-enthusiastic!

Where Murphy and Brannagan had gone down for life, the judge sentenced the real culprits to five years. Why such discrepancy? Did Baron Pollock regard burglary and shooting two people less seriously than Justice Manisty? Or did Justice Manisty consider his father would have been the 'injured party' had the burglary been committed when he was vicar at Edlingham, and allow his feelings to interfere with his judgement?

Peter Murphy and Michael Brannagan were freed, their pardons signed by Queen Victoria. They each received £800 compensation, a considerable sum then. But no amount of money can compensate for false accusation and loss of liberty. In prison they had each learned a trade, Murphy as a baker, Brannagan as a wheelwright, so at least their poaching days were over.

There remained the matter of corrupt policemen. Four constables were charged with making false plaster casts of footprints, conning Redpath into 'identifying' the chisel, tearing a piece of newspaper in the vicarage and 'planting' the matching piece into what they believed to be Murphy's jacket and cutting off a piece from Brannagan's corduroy trousers, and leaving it at the scene as proof he had been there. Why the constables alone stood in the dock for conspiracy you might wonder. What about the main protagonist, Superintendent Harkes?

Harkes it was who led this disgraceful sequence of events. From the start he seemed convinced he had the right men and had the power to fashion the evidence to prove it. Unfortunately he died two years before the truth emerged and so escaped a conviction for conspiracy. The other officers escaped too, every one. They were 'obeying orders', so walked free. Would they have done so had Mr Buckle or his daughter died that night? No-one will ever know.

Point to Ponder

An Englishman's home is his castle, so it is said. So when two intruders forcibly entered the vicarage home of the Rev Buckle that night in 1879 he would consider he had every right to arm himself with his sword before setting off in the darkness to challenge them. As well as protecting himself and his property, he had his invalid wife and daughter to consider, and four female servants, all imperilled by the danger lurking downstairs.

But would he have this right today, when people are sent to prison for defending their property? 'Reasonable force' is the maxim, and each case is subjective. But at night, awakened by unknown men, how can one know what 'reasonable force' is? Are they armed? If so, with what? New laws look at the 'human rights' of offenders, not victims. If the Edlingham burglary took place today, the Rev Buckle would do well to think twice before taking up his sword and risk causing injury to those who would enter his home.

Murdered On His Beat

Six years before the burglary at Edlingham vicarage, Charles Richardson stood trial for shooting and killing a policeman, PC George Grey, at Eglingham, also near Alnwick.

PC Grey, 41, married with four children, had been on his beat, a quiet country road, about three o'clock one morning when he encountered three poachers who ran into a field pursued by the constable. From less than 20 yards one of them raised a shotgun, shooting the officer in the chest and abdomen. Hearing the shot, four men left their beds, ran into the field and carried PC Grey into nearby Glebe Cottage. Later that day PC Grey died of gunshot wounds to his lungs, heart, liver, stomach and intestines. The sum of £86 was collected for his wife and four orphaned children, and a reward of £300 was put on the heads of his killers.

As in the Edlingham case, police took plaster casts of footprints, found in the soil where the men had been. One was very distinctive, made by a boot with a 'slit heel plate' and with a sole studded with square-headed nails. Insp Harrison went to the tile works on Alnwick Moor where he confronted Charles Richardson. One of Richardson's boots corresponded to the impressions in the soil. A

Eglingham: the Tankerville Arms, on PC George Grey's beat.

few weeks earlier Insp Harrison had seen Richardson with a gun, and asked to see it now. Richardson showed him another. When charged with the murder of PC Grey he replied, 'I am innocent as the babe unborn.'

Two other men were arrested, including George Edgell, a running mate of Richardson's. They were ne're-do-wells who carried arms. All walked free, save Richardson, who alone stood trial. He too walked free. The foot impression found by police had been protected against rain that had fallen before the plaster casts could be made, but was not considered 'safe'. The gun was never found. Charles Richardson and George Edgell were free to commit crime later, as they did at the Edlingham vicarage.

Eglingham Church, situated in a quiet backwater.

SHOT IN COLD BLOOD

Memorial to two murdered policemen,
Bedlington cemetery.

The murder of police officers in this country has always been a rare event. Even today patrolling police men and women are unarmed, save for a few in special circumstances. The constable who deals with the incident on the street, or attends the location where there is 'trouble', will ordinarily carry no more than a truncheon or side baton. On Tuesday, 15th April, 1913, PC George Bertram Mussell and Sergeant Andrew Barton, stationed at Bedlington, were unarmed coppers who were shot dead in cold blood by an enraged gunman who also took the life of an innocent woman, Sarah Ellen Fenwick Grice.

He was John Vickers Amos, a 35-year old married man with three children, who at the time was licensee of the Sun Inn on the town's main street. Far from having a reputation as a thug or someone who lived outside the law, Jocker, as he was known, was a peaceful chap who had no reputation for harming anyone. Yet he killed three innocent people who meant him no harm. Why?

Jocker was nothing if not a hard working, industrious character. A miner since he was 12, four times in seven years he had gone to Alabama, where he reputedly saved workmates in two mining

The Sun Inn, Bedlington.

Mrs Sarah Grice, murdered by Jocker Amos.

accidents. Then he was in a mining explosion that killed two men, after which he had suffered, not surprisingly, you might think, from stress and severe headaches. Returning to England, he was taken on as landlord at the Sun Inn, using his hard-earned £30 savings as a bond to secure the tenancy. He was popular with the locals, with his tales of his experiences in the States.

Unfortunately, where he excelled as congenial host, his bookeeping ability was a disaster. At least, that's what the owner, Mr James Wood Irons, would say. Jocker took over at the Sun Inn in January, 1913, and a month later when Irons did a stock check he told Amos there was a shortfall of £7 5s 0d. Jocker protested, saying every penny taken had gone into the till. A fortnight later Irons did another stock check, finding the discrepancy had risen to £21 11s 0d, and on 6th April it stood at £45 19s 5d. This was unacceptable to James Irons who gave Amos until 15th April to set things right.

Came the day. Irons arrived with a professional stocktaker and it must have been obvious to Jocker that he was out. So he was. Indeed his replacement, Mr Richard Grice and his wife, Sarah, were to take over that very day. When Jocker enquired about the return of his bond, Irons told him it depended on the stocktake.

One can feel the pressure Jocker Amos must have been under, especially if he had not been 'on the fiddle' and there was an explanation, albeit one he could not give, about the shortfall. His experiences in America may well have put him on a short fuse as far as reacting to stress was concerned. In any event, as the stock was being checked, Mrs Amos happened to appear at the top of the stairs carrying Jocker's Winchester shotgun, saying a customer had asked to borrow it to go shooting. Jocker said the gun was not going anywhere and sent his son to buy some cartridges. 'Do you think I went to the States to work hard for Mr Irons to take my money?' he said to a servant girl.

Jocker bolted the back door of the inn and shouted at Irons, 'We'll see who's boss here', to which Irons reacted by going to the police station where he saw Inspector Culley who said he'd send a constable along. A pale reaction, you might think, when the inspector was told a man about to be thrown out of his home with his family was in possession of a gun and had just sent for ammunition.

Irons collected Mr Grice from the railway station and they went to the inn. The atmosphere was getting worse as the time was approaching when Jocker and his family would have to quit. Foreseeing trouble, Irons returned to police station and requested the attendance of a constable, as promised. Constable George Mussell was assigned, first accompanying Irons to Sleekburn where they met Mrs Grice who was waiting with a cartload of family possessions.

The party proceeded to the Sun, arriving around three o'clock. PC Mussell waited as the stocktaker completed his task after which Irons gave Jocker two weeks' wages – £3 – and told to him to get out, and take his family and possessions with him. Clearly Irons would not be returning the bond. This was all too much for Jocker, who went upstairs and appeared in the corridor carrying the shotgun. PC Mussell confronted him. One can imagine the scene, the constable saying 'come on Jocker', as he tried to reason with someone he knew. Jocker's response was to discharge both barrels into PC Mussell's chest and neck, killing him instantly.

Hearing the shots, Irons fled through the cellar hatchway. Mrs Grice, appeared at a downstairs window, screaming 'save me, save me', but Amos shot her in the back of the head and she too died instantly, tumbling down the cellar steps. Then a friend of the Grice's, Mrs Craggs, appeared from the cellar with her children, a girl, 17 and a young boy, and all found themselves facing the now-demented Amos. Mrs Craggs begged him to spare her on account of the children, and he mercifully let them go without harm.

The gunshots were heard by a number of people outside, including Sergeant Andrew Barton. He and others ran to the inn, and the sergeant entered without hesitation, finding PC Mussell's body the bottom of the stairs. He knew the score as he confronted Jocker, and stood his ground before the barrels of Jocker's gun as he tried to persuade him to give himself up. Sergeant Barton had a proven track record for bravery; he won a medal for gallantry when he swam through stormy seas to

Inscription on the memorial to Sgt Barton and PC Mussell.

rescue a sailor off Warkworth six years before. Jocker shot him dead on the spot. Others who had ventured into the inn fled in fear of their lives.

Whilst one cannot doubt the bravery of Sergeant Barton especially, one wonders why he did not hesitate. In the knowledge that Amos was armed and had killed his colleague and Mrs Grice, why did he step forward and forfeit his own life? Did he feel it his duty, no matter what? Or did he believe Amos could be persuaded to see sense? Northumberland was the last county in England to form a police force. Its citizens can be proud of the two officers who died at Bedlington that day.

Irons, meantime, had returned to the police station where Inspector Culley, belatedly, sent for reinforcements. At the Sun, Jocker kept appearing at the door, brandishing the gun. Finally he lit a cigarette, telling the crowd which had gathered there were two cartridges in the gun, one for him, the other for anyone who ventured near. Senior police officers, including the chief constable, arrived, and there was a 'stand off' situation for a time until Jocker decided it was time to go. He left by the back door, took to the fields and disappeared.

Armed police and armed civilians searched for Amos. It was dusk when Joe Potter, a miner, saw a footprint in the grass near a culvert beneath a road. A police inspector told Potter to fire a round into the culvert. Nothing happened. A second shot was discharged, this time followed by a cry of pain and Jocker emerged, pellets having grazed his forehead. He was arrested and taken to the police station. His gun had jammed, which was the reason he didn't shoot himself or anyone else.

The bodies of the two dead officers were taken to the police station, Mrs Grice rested at the Sun Inn; it was to have been her home, instead it was her mortuary. Jocker Amos's trial at Newcastle Assizes commenced at the Moot Hall, on 2nd July. He was charged with killing all three persons at the Sun Inn but evidence of only one killing, that of Sergeant Barton, was heard. Murder was a capital crime, and you can only hang a man once. He pleaded not guilty.

Prosecuting counsel, Mr Williamson, set out to prove 'life had been taken deliberately and intentionally'. After hearing of the tragedies on the fateful day, James Wood Irons, the owner of the Sun Inn, testified.

The police force of old.

He had made it clear, he said, that he had never accused Jocker Amos or his wife of stealing money, but that he held Jocker responsible, whatever the reason for the shortfall. Mr Waugh, defending, said Amos had lost his mental balance; he said that Mr Irons had driven a hard bargain: the high price he put on a barrel of beer meant the manager was bound to show a stock deficiency of £1 day, and the more beer Amos sold, the more barrels he would require and the greater would be the loss to Amos and the greater would be the profit to Irons.

But none of this could justify murder and the judge said that Amos was fully aware of the fateful consequences of his actions; both policemen had tried to take his gun and he had shot them, and killing Mrs Grice was 'most mysterious'. It took the jury eight minutes to find Jocker guilty. The judge asked him if he had anything to say. 'I don't remember anything,' said Jocker, 'they were good friends to me.' He meant, of course, the policemen who died trying to help him and uphold the law. His defence was that he was insane at the time he killed them. Surely he was.

Over 60,000 people signed a petition, asking the Home Secretary to commute the sentence. Those who signed it were not against the death penalty but believed in this case it was not merited. Hadn't Amos suffered tragedy in America? Didn't he have a wife and three children? And that Irons chap, he wasn't whiter than white, was he? Their plea was refused, yet even as Amos, triple murderer, sat in his cell, his former colleagues, the miners, themselves rallied to his cause. At the Northumberland Miners' Picnic they passed a resolution calling for mercy, which was telegraphed to the Home Secretary and even the King. There would be no reprieve and Jocker Amos, like many before him, turned to God. He was baptised and in a letter to his father he wrote 'I will put myself in the Lord's hands'. He went quietly to the gallows at Newcastle gaol on 22nd July.

The following January the murdered officers' wives each received the King's Police Medal. The citation read: 'Both officers, disregarding the consequences to themselves, advanced to their duty and in doing so met their deaths. Their behaviour affords an example to those now serving and to all who may join the force in years to come'. Their widows received no pension. Of his treatment by police and prison officers, Jocker Amos declared he had been treated like a gentleman. It seems he died like one.

Point to Ponder

Was Jocker Amos a wicked man? Did he plan to kill an innocent woman and two police officers who, by his own admission, were his friends? Was he in his right mind when he did? He murdered using a firearm, not because he wanted to, but because he was able to.

A loaded gun means power. Power to exert one's will. Power to brush aside reason. And, in the hands of someone who is cracking under strain, power to act irrationally and indiscriminately. Carrying a gun changes a man. From the need to act with caution, he can act with aggression. From being unable to easily harm others, he can destroy in an instant. Years ago, firearms were more readily available than today; they were used mainly in hunting, and Jocker Amos had no problem sending his son over the road to buy the ammunition.

Perhaps the only way to prevent the tragedies of Bedlington and latterly, Hungerford and Dunblane, is to make guns inaccessible, including to the law-abiding public. Jocker Amos was law-abiding till something went wrong with his rationale. Even gangsters who possess guns outside the law would not have murdered so indiscriminately. As a matter of fact, with certain rare exceptions, they usually murder each other.

A Mysterious Affair

Not all killers were hanged pre-1965. Some weren't caught, others had the death sentence commuted to life imprisonment. Still others took their own lives before the law could intervene. The man or woman who commits suicide may or may not be rational, but one thing is certain: there is no easy way. There may be pain, trauma or even failure, and it is doubtful that they ever consider the feelings of their families nor, indeed, the feelings of anyone but themselves. Thomas Jobling, 25, was a labourer who lodged with John Ebbelwhite and his family at North Walbottle. Mr Ebblewhite's daughter, Jane, 18, was 'in domestic service' with Isaiah Wilson, three doors away. Ebblewhite was engineman at North Walbottle Colliery.

On Sunday evening, 7th September, 1902, Jane and Thomas Jobling went for a walk. They were seen about 6.45 p.m. in an area of open country known as the Bogs, about a mile from the village, by Elizabeth Hewitson. She saw Jobling try to put his arm around Jane's waist. She resisted at first, then consented, and they walked to a stile which Jobling climbed over but Jane refused, sitting down on the step instead. Nothing of either's conduct or demeanour gave Mrs Hewitson cause to think that anything was amiss. Joseph Taylor, of Throckley, saw the couple twice. Once, about 8 p.m. near Callerton, again three quarters of an hour later. On each occasion

North Walbottle Colliery. Also known as 'High Pit', it closed in 1968.

they were arm in arm. Jobling had told Taylor he wanted to marry Jane so Taylor was not surprised to see them out together. He could not have known he would be the last person to see Jane Ebblewhite alive.

The next time anyone saw Jane was just after midnight when John Reddy, one of a search party, looked over a wall in the Bogs area. The first thing he spotted was Jane's hat, then he found a man's collar and tie and a pair of cufflinks. Farther on he saw an elbow protruding from the surface of the Dewley Burn. It was Jane, lying face down in the water. She had been strangled by a handkerchief which was tied tightly around her neck, and was fully clothed. The local constable, PC Purvis, attended and arranged for her body to be taken to her father's house. Returning to the Bogs, he found the grass trampled where there had been a struggle. It seemed Jane's body was dragged over the grass and left in the burn.

About 9.40 p.m. on that fateful Sunday evening, William Start was on duty at the pit when Thomas Jobling appeared and called out 'Is Ebblewhite here?', meaning was Jane's father in the engine room. 'No,' Stark called back. A minute later he found Jobling at the top of the shaft, inside the gates, in 'an excited condition'. Stark told him to leave but Jobling jumped down the shaft. Isaiah Wilson was standing at the shaft bottom when Jobling landed on top of the cage. The force of the impact broke his body into two pieces. 'A horrible death', the coroner would say, returning a verdict of suicide.

We shall never know what went on between Thomas Jobling and Jane that evening. Suffice to say for whatever reason he murdered her and took his own life. One wonders if he would have killed himself if murder had not carried the death penalty, if instead he would have been sentenced to life imprisonment in the knowledge that he would be free one day. We shall never know that either.

MURDER ON THE TRAIN

The victim: John Nisbet.

The man they hanged: John Alexander Dickman.

For twenty years, John Nisbet had made the journey on alternate Fridays: Newcastle to Widdrington Station on the Alnmouth train, taking the wages for miners at Stobswood Colliery. The money, in cash, he carried in a small, locked leather bag. You could do that in those days, it seemed, without fear of molestation, a routine task for which Mr Nisbet would have neither required nor expected the need for security.

Friday, 18th March, 1910, was no different. Mr Nisbet turned up at Newcastle Central Station to catch the 10.27 train. He was seen and recognised on Platform 5 by at least three people who knew him, Percival Hall and John Spink, two men who were bound for Stannington on a similar mission, albeit to a different colliery, and Charles Raven. Unusually, Nisbet was in company with another man, whom Raven knew by sight but not by name, but whom Hall and Spink did not know. The man was wearing a light overcoat. Hall saw Nisbet and the unknown man board the train together, occupying the same carriage but a different compartment to himself and Spink.

The carriage comprised three compartments: the first acted as 'bogey brake'; the middle one was occupied by Nesbit and the unknown man, whilst Hall and Spink sat in the third and last

---

JOURNAL, SATURDAY, MARCH 19, 1910.

HOURS TROUBLE.
:o:

of Trade Conference to be Held.

IMBERLAND MINERS' DEPUTATION.

with the coal trade trouble in fresh hope of a settlement has active interest which the Board ing in the dispute. The main ute over the Eight Hours Act lready been communicated to ind now Mr Askwith, the head Statistical Section, has asked lisaffected men have to say. corresponding secretary of the , has forwarded the following etaries of the lodges where

Newcastle, March 16, 1910. g the running of the disputes which have not commenced county agreement, there has

RAILWAY TRAGEDY.
:o:

Newcastle Clerk Murdered

ROBBERY OF £370 IN GOLD.

Intended as Pitmen's Pay at Stobswood.

MYSTERIOUS CIRCUMSTANCES.

A cold-blooded and evidently premeditated murder, with robbery as the motive, took place in a train between Newcastle and Alnwick yesterday.

When the 10.27 a.m. train from Newcastle and the south arrived shortly after mid-day at Alnmouth Station, where the tickets were collected, the foreman porter noticed an empty compartment which had its window down. Opening the door to put the window up he saw a pool of blood

field of th Alnmouth,

Though the part of to a late h

The dec Quayside, by the firr boy, a pe office of t boy, he r held the alternativ been par from the there. for this The ch £370 9s in the yesterda cashier He cash Station. 10.27 a. Mr N was the

---

Newcastle Journal, 19th March, 1910: Railway Tragedy.

compartment. They were seated in the first carriage, unusually for Nisbet, whose wife customarily turned up at Heaton Station to acknowledge her husband when the train stopped briefly there. On this occasion she was surprised to find him further along the train and had to run to tell him through the window to be 'home by six'. She noticed another man in the compartment, but not clearly. Hall and Spink left the train at Stannington when the former nodded politely to Nisbet, who was seated facing the engine. The unknown man sat opposite and was not well seen. The next time anyone saw Nisbet was at Alnmouth, at the end of the line, when a porter found his body pushed under the seat, in a pool of blood. He had been shot five times through the head.

It seems certain that Nisbet was murdered between Stannington and Morpeth, the next station, six minutes further up the line. This is borne out by the evidence of a passenger named Grant, who boarded at

Alnmouth: the end of the line for John Nisbet.

Morpeth where he found the middle compartment of the first carriage apparently empty. Grant did not enter, but sat elsewhere. The recovered bullets were probably all discharged from the same weapon. The motive was clearly robbery, for the cash bag and its contents were missing. The money, amounting to £370 9s 6d, was made up of approximately 400 sovereigns and half-sovereigns, silver and copper. The killer would have left the train at Morpeth, carrying a small but heavy parcel.

John Innes Nisbet was an innocent man going about his daily business. Described as a 'genial, kind-hearted man', he was 44 years old with two children. The company offered £100 reward to any person 'not being the actual murderer' who could give information to discovery and conviction of the murderer. Police in Northumberland and Newcastle began their hunt for the unknown assassin, and a description was circulated of a man, 30 to 40 years, 5' 6", with a black or brown moustache, wearing a light overcoat and black felt hat and appearing 'fairly well-to-do.' This description fitted about half the male population at the time.

Alnmouth Station today.

John Nisbet wasn't the only person recognised by passengers on the train at Newcastle Central Station. An artist, William Hepple, seated in the last carriage, recognised John Alexander Dickman, whom he had known for years, walking towards the front of the train with another man whom he did not recognise – Nisbet, presumably. It seems they boarded the train. When the story of the murder broke Hepple contacted the police and mentioned Dickman as a possible witness. On this basis Detective Inspector Tait called to see Dickman at his home in Jesmond. Dickman confirmed he had seen Nisbet at the Central Station, and that he had known him for years. They had booked their tickets at the same time but had not travelled in the same carriage, he said.

He was taken to Newcastle police station where he made a written statement. In it, he said he had travelled in the last carriage, intending to get off the train at Stannington. Thanks to being engrossed in the racing page of his newspaper he had missed the station and gone on to Morpeth, and paid an excess fare of 2½d (later verified). The purpose of his journey was to go to Dovecot Colliery, near Stannington, to see a Mr Hogg and ask him for a small loan. Having reached Morpeth he'd set off on foot, but on the way he had taken ill with diarrhoea so he decided to return to Newcastle. He retraced steps to Morpeth where, having missed the next train, he went walkabout and encountered a Mr Elliott, whom he knew, near the station. Elliott would say that Dickman appeared composed, and talked of horseracing; he noticed no bloodstains about his clothing.

Dickman's account did not tally with Hepple's – who stated Dickman had walked to the front carriage – and he was arrested. His house was searched but there was no trace of any weapon or the stolen cash bag or its contents. Police did find a pair or bloodstained suede gloves and trousers; Dickman said the bloodstains had been there for a long period. They also found some pawn tickets in the name of 'John Wilkinson'. They discovered that Dickman had an arrangement at a business premises in Newcastle, whereby letters sent to him in the name 'A. Black' could be collected. The previous October a parcel had arrived from a firm of gunsmiths, addressed to him in that name. When Dickman hadn't called to collect it the company had sent a postcard asking for 'the return of the revolver', after which he collected the parcel.

Evidence of identification was crucial and would be the only hard evidence. Dickman admitted being at the station and boarding the train. Who could put them in the same carriage as Nisbet, thereby proving he was the killer?

Percival Hall had said he could pick the man 'out of a dozen'. Now came his opportunity. He and John Spink attended the police station to try and identify Dickman on a police 'line up' of about nine persons. Hall, looking Dickman over, declared, 'If it is any one of these, it is he.' A somewhat dubious identification, to say the least. There appears to be no record about Spink in this regard, but at least the police had one 'positive' identification. Mrs Nisbet, making a second statement after her appearance at the magistrates' court remand hearing during which she fainted said, 'The little I saw of the man in the train that day he had his coat collar up and it partly covered his face. I recognised the same part of his face in the dock the other day'!

Dickman had financial problems. Suffice to say he had little money – £17 when arrested, a not inconsiderable sum then but that might have been part of the stolen cash. He had borrowed money and pawned some cheap jewellery in desperation – for money, the prosecution would say, to prevent it being stolen by burglars, said Dickman, an unlikely story it has to be said. In any event, Dickman, when charged with murder, replied, 'I only say I absolutely deny it.'

An interesting discovery was made in the compartment occupied by Nesbit and his killer. Bloody finger-marks were found on a leather-bound armrest of the seat where Nisbet had been sitting. The material was sent to London for examination by experts. Unfortunately, nothing could be made of it. Whose finger impressions were they? A porter's, possibly, for the whole seat had been removed. The killer's, probably, as it was made in keeping with someone resting his hand there while dragging the body on to the floor. But that didn't prove Dickman was the killer.

A commercial traveller, Mr Brocklehurst stated that a fortnight previously he and others were travelling by train from Newcastle to Morpeth when they were startled by a noise that sounded like a revolver. Letting down the carriage window and looking out they saw

Lord Coleridge, the judge in the Dickman case.

the framework outside the window splintered, apparently by bullets fired by a person in another compartment. Had shots been fired from outside the train they would have gone into the compartment. This might account for the killer choosing a forward carriage, where the sound of a gunshot would be drowned out by the sound of the engine. But was it Dickman?

On 9th June, about a month before the trial, Peter Spooner, manager at the Isabella Pit, near Hepscott, found the cash bag Nisbet had carried lying at the bottom of a disused mineshaft, having been slipped through the iron bars. The bag had been cut open and now contained only a few coins. Two important factors now presented themselves: Dickman and Spooner were acquainted, having spoken about the difficulties of working the pit due to water, so Dickman would probably be acquainted with the disused shaft. And Dickman could have reached the colliery on foot and returned to Morpeth on the day of the murder. In other words, his walkabout and being taken ill was a red herring to account for the time taken in disposing of the evidence.

Came the trial at Newcastle Assizes, presided over by Lord Coleridge. Tindal Atkinson, was counsel for the Crown, Edward Mitchell-Innes for Dickman. No witness was called for the defence, save Dickman himself. He stated his proposed visit to Dovecote Colliery was not by appointment so he would not have been expected. He admitted being an ex-secretary at a colliery company and that he knew wages to colliery employees were paid on alternate Fridays. He admitted making previous journeys on the same train. Were they made ostensibly to see Mr Hogg, at Dovecote, or for more sinister reasons – to ascertain where the train was noisiest, perhaps, where a gunshot might not be heard?

Technology in those days was far less advanced than now, and the blood on Dickman's suede gloves and trousers could not be matched with Nisbet's. Dr Boland could not even say if it was human blood but confirmed it was not more than two weeks old, not several months, as Dickman suggested.

Then came a blunder by prosecution counsel, alluding to the fact that Dickman's wife had not been called upon to give evidence. She was not obliged to, but what is significant is that under the law prosecution counsel was not permitted to comment on this. Tindal Atkinson admitted, when the matter was raised by the defence, that he had done so in 'pure inadvertence and forgetfulness'. Here was a man on trial for his life and the jury hearing matters barred by law. Yet the judge allowed it to stand. Today, I suggest, the case against Dickman would be thrown out or a retrial ordered, if not by the judge then and there, then by the Court of Appeal. It was permitted to stand, a clear injustice against the defendant.

No murder weapon recovered, no stolen property recovered, save for the cash bag and a few coins, no forensic evidence, and no admission to the crime. There was, at least, the evidence of the positive identification of Dickman, although the witness Hepple was the sole person who would say he saw Dickman go to the front of the train, as well as Dickman's implausible story of how he spent his time having got off the train in Morpeth. He was a man in need of money, a man who had evidently taken possession of a revolver through the post.

The judge apologised to the jury for the mistake by Mr Atkinson, but the fact was they'd heard it. When the jury returned, the judge asked if this had been allowed to 'affect them'. 'We have not mentioned it,' said the foreman. The verdict was guilty. After sentence of death Dickman addressed the court from the dock, saying 'I declare to all men, I am innocent.'

Dickman was doomed, but there is more to tell of this tale, not least that between the trial and the date of Dickman's appeal, thanks to information provided by the chief constable who somehow must have got wind, it transpired that when Hall and Spink had attended the police station for the identification line up a constable suggested they might care to take a peek through the window of the room where Dickman was to see if they could recognise him. The window being partly of frosted glass they did not have a view of his face, so they were

An engraving of Newcastle Prison.

afforded the opportunity to look through a partly-open doorway where they saw a man in a light overcoat. Minutes later they would see the same man on the line up and would have no problem in recognising him as one and the same. Whether or not it was the man on the train on the day of the crime cannot be known. This 'identification' must have affected the jury's decision.

After the trial, it transpired Mrs Nisbet had known Dickman by sight for years. So her identification, such as it was, was worthless, for she merely identified someone she knew and the police had in custody. Why didn't she say so? Was she asked not to by the police? Despite these developments on the crucial issue of identification, the appeal court declined to intervene. And still that is not the end of the story, for it seems John Dickman was also fancied for two other murders, that of a moneylender at Sunderland the year before, a man named Cohen who was beaten to death in his office when money from the safe and a diamond ring were stolen (the victim's finger being cut off in the process), and of a Mrs Luard, who was shot dead outside her home near Sevenoaks, Kent, on 24th August, 1908. The latter case raises serious issues over the Dickman trial.

Dickman met Mrs Luard on the matter of a cheque she had sent to him in response to an advertisement in a newspaper. Dickman had allegedly forged the cheque. Major-General Luard, Mrs Luard's husband, committed suicide the day after his wife's murder, possibly because of anonymous letters he had had received, suggesting he was the killer. Mr Luard was a personal friend of certain members of the judiciary, notably Lord Coleridge, the trial judge in the Dickman case, and every member of the appeal court, which had ignored the flawed evidence of identification. As if that wasn't enough, the Home Secretary, Winston Churchill, whose duty it was to consider commuting the death sentence to life imprisonment, was a personal friend of Major-General Luard! Good friends in high places do not make for sound justice.

John Alexander Dickman was hanged in Newcastle on 10th August, 1910, despite a petition asking for clemency and another signed by five members of the jury requesting the same (did they, after all, doubt his guilt?). Just before his execution, he was asked by the prison chaplain if he 'would die with a lie on his lips.' In other words, if he would care to admit to the crime. This was common enough; many men admitted the crime when death stared them in the face, when they had nothing to lose and everything to gain in the eyes of the Lord. 'I'm saying nothing,' said Dickman. When the hangman, Ellis, pinioned his hands, Dickman declared he would not die with his coat on. So Ellis, sensing trouble, removed the strap and permitted Dickman to take off his jacket. This was unusual, for hanging someone was a fast-track procedure, something to be done quickly and without fuss. Having got his way, Dickman, again pinioned, stepped up to the gallows and without a word went to his doom.

Point to Ponder

One wonders whether the case was sufficiently proven against John Dickman. There seems to be little doubt that he was guilty – although, let it be said, 'little doubt' is not the criteria to secure guilt, rather the law requires the case to be proved 'beyond reasonable doubt'. But Dickman's trial was not fair.

The evidence of identification was flawed, thanks to cheating by the police. If it wasn't revealed at the trial, as it wasn't, it was known about by the time the case came to appeal yet their Lordships failed to consider it. The only witness who pointed the finger at Dickman was the artist, William Hepple. No-one save he said it was Dickman who walked along the platform with John Nisbet.

Taken as a whole, the circumstances of this case tend to show Dickman did murder John Nisbet. Yet, having regard to the flawed evidence of identification and the cosy club consisting of the trial judge, the appeal court judges – every one – and even the Home Secretary, one cannot say the man had a fair trial, or a fair appeal hearing. The judge's knowledge that the accused was suspected of murdering the wife of his friend, whose husband subsequently committed suicide, and similarly all the appeal court judges and even the Home Secretary, meant they could not have been seen to be impartial.

If John Alexander Dickman did not have a fair trial, he ought not to have been convicted.

Who's That Lady?

On Tuesday, 22nd March, 1910, crowds turned out at two places – Jesmond cemetery, at the funeral of Mr Nisbet, and Gosforth court, for the appearance of John Dickman before the magistrate, Richard Welford. Naturally, Mrs Dickman was present. She wore a smart, grey costume and a hat whose feathers, described as 'resembling a guinea fowl', were the predominant feature.

When one of the reporters present started to sketch proceedings, including, presumably, Mrs Dickman, resplendent in her hat, she rose and went over to him. 'I object to you sketching,' she said. The reporter closed his book, saying 'sorry.' But Mrs Dickman wasn't finished. As the prosecution commenced she said out loud, 'And I object to any description being given of me.'

'Who is that lady?' asked the magistrate. Mr Clark, Dickman's solicitor, told him, adding, out loud, presumably for the benefit of his client's wife, 'I don't think they are taking sketches. If they do they generally murder them and no-one can recognise anybody.' An apt description, in the circumstances. Perhaps Mrs Dickman needed more convincing for she turned her chair around and sat with her back to the reporters. Meanwhile, her husband was in the dock to answer to a charge of murder.

John Alexander Dickman at his trial.

BUTCHERED BY A 'MONSTER'

Matheson is brought to Newcastle police station by detectives.

John Neil, a probationer constable stationed at Glasgow's main police station, might not have thought much to the man in the shabby raincoat standing at the enquiry desk that quiet Saturday afternoon. Until, that is, he announced he had come 'to give himself up'. The constable telephoned CID and might have been killed in the rush as three detective sergeants arrived to arrest Albert Matheson, 52, the most wanted man in Britain.

Matheson's particulars had been circulated following the murder of fifteen-year old Gordon Lockhart of High Heaton, Newcastle. Gordon had only left school that August, and on Monday, 18th November, 1957, had started as trainee projectionist at the Pavilion cinema, Westgate Road, Newcastle. But when he left the building on a tea break that afternoon he was never seen alive again.

Gordon's mother, Mrs Evelyn Lockhart, reported her son missing just after midnight. Police using dogs searched derelict buildings and allotments, but there was no sign of Gordon. The police had every right to be concerned for there had been sightings of a stranger, a shabbily dressed man seen talking to Gordon and even hanging around his house on the day before he started work at the Pavilion. What's more, Mrs Lockhart had received three postcards. The first, signed 'G.S.',

How the *Journal* reported the murder of Gordon Lockhart, November, 1957.

Victim of Murder: 15-year old
Gordon Lockhart.

received on Wednesday, said 'Gordon has gone to London as a woman
is after him for money to keep his baby'. The following day came the
second: 'Gordon is living with prostitutes' and purported to come from
an old school pal, who added that Gordon had borrowed £1 from him
and gone to London. The third said, simply, 'Gordon is dead'.

So he was. But one can scarcely imagine the feelings of his mother
and his family who were left wondering if it was true, or the cruel
work of a madman. The police in turn wondered if it could be the work
of a suspect they had identified: Albert Matheson, who worked as a
handyman at the St James's Boxing Hall, near St James's Park. Police
made a thorough search of the hall, and Gordon Lockhart's body was
discovered in a sump underneath the boxing ring. He had sustained
head injuries, consistent with being attacked with a bottle, and his
body had been cut in two. Parts of his remains were found in a kitbag
close by. His body was clothed, but his shoes were missing. Later,
evidence that 'a sexual offence had taken place' would be given.

Police checked Matheson's lodgings but he had flown. His
description, including, unusually, his name and picture (so certain
were the police of their man) was circulated to other forces and the

media. The stranger who had been seen hanging around and later was discovered to have called at the Pavilion enquiring about Gordon fitted Matheson's description: 'bald with a little silver hair on top of his head, five feet six, of thin build with a sunken face and several teeth missing'. That he had been seen near Gordon's home indicated the two had become acquainted by that time. In fact, Matheson had fled to Edinburgh where he stayed in an hotel under the name 'George Small, Newcastle'. After his arrest, when he produced a newspaper cutting showing a photograph of Gordon Lockhart, police searched his room where they found Gordon's shoes wrapped in a brown paper parcel, addressed to Mrs Lockhart.

Matheson's crime was in Newcastle, and when he was brought south two lines of police had to keep back the crowds who had flocked to see him on his court appearance before the magistrates. The public were kept from the court, although members of the Lockhart family were admitted. Two of Gordon's brothers had to be restrained by police as they tried to climb over the rail to the dock. Matheson was remanded in custody as the police began to put the evidence together to prove their case.

And evidence there was aplenty. Matheson, a homosexual, told the magistrates at a later hearing that Gordon Lockhart had had £35 in his possession. 'I took the money out of his pocket,' he said, 'that's why I

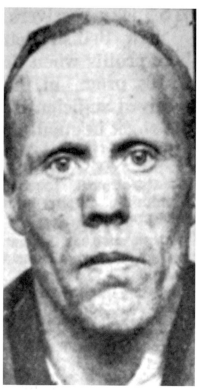

Albert Edward Matheson. He
fled to Scotland.

St James's Boxing & Wrestling Hall is no more … Today the site is occupied by the St James's Metro station, towered over by the new football stadium.

killed him.' He said Gordon got the money off 'a businessman' in Jesmond, but refused to name him. He said Gordon had shown him the money. 'I hit him with the beer bottle and he would not give it to me so I hit him on the head with a hammer.'

There is clear direction in the police line of questioning here. At the time, a murderer could not hang unless the murder was committed in connection with certain laid-down offences, including (as in this case, the police said) the furtherance of theft – a so-called capital crime. To have murdered, say, in the course of an unlawful homosexual act would not be a capital offence (homosexual acts were unlawful then, even between consenting parties). By admitting murdering for money, Matheson was lining himself up for the gallows.

Matheson told police he had hidden Gordon's body overnight before dumping him in the well, or sump, underneath the boxing ring. There were plenty of blood-stained walls to bear out this testimony. The post mortem examination revealed 25 penetrating wounds to the scalp; death was due to multiple head injuries. He admitted sending the cards to Gordon's mother, and two letters, postmarked Edinburgh – one on the back of a calendar with a picture of a mother and baby, on which had written, 'Your son was a homosexual maniac … Was he like this as a baby? The remains are in the River Tyne'; the other was to the chief constable of Newcastle City Police: 'Have you found that body yet? It is in pieces in the River Tyne in sacks'. An expert confirmed the similarity in the handwriting (insofar as his evidence was not challenged; such 'expert' opinion rarely stands up to scrutiny unlike, say, fingerprint evidence).

Matheson, you might think, was a man so deranged he was neither fit to plead or be at large in the community. He was described in a prison report as 'a sexual pervert' – although one must be guarded here, as homosexuals in those days were by and large all considered 'perverted' – and in declining medical treatment had asked to be castrated. Over the years, he had attempted suicide on numerous occasions by swallowing razor blades, needles and pieces of wire. To save his life, he'd had seven operations on his stomach.

There was yet more evidence to prove Matheson's association with Gordon Lockhart. A cleaner at the Pavilion, Agnes Bartlett, said at 9 a.m. on the day Gordon started work there, Matheson had been asking for him, saying he was a friend; and Kenneth Turner, the projectionist, said Matheson had said he had a message for Gordon, and that later, at 4.30 p.m. Gordon had gone for tea and had not returned. George Robert Welch, the manager of St James's Boxing Hall, said he had engaged Matheson as a handyman on 8th November. Matheson had a key to the dressing room, and a claw hammer he was shown was normally kept in there.

Matheson, when the charge was read over to him at the magistrates' court, stood up sharply and said, 'I do not want to be represented at the Assizes.' When he did appear, the following January, Dr Ian Pickering, Senior Medical Officer at Durham Prison, told the court, 'Matheson is obsessed with his sexual perversion, and any conversation with him reverts to the same topic.' He said he had formed the opinion that Matheson 'was one of those unstable individuals who are classed as psychopathic personalities'. He said that in his opinion 'he knew what he was doing'.

Dr Robert Orton, consultant psychiatrist, said that he found Matheson 'dull, with no feeling for anyone else'. He went on, 'I feel that he has no ability to understand right and wrong, and that on impulse he tends to do something which pleases him without any hope for the future or the consequences of his behaviour. He suffers from an abnormality of mind. He is without doubt a psychopathic personality, an individual of feeble intelligence'. Dr Theodore Cuthbert, consultant psychiatrist, said he found Matheson to have a development of mind expected of someone less than the age of ten who had not grown up and that he didn't think he had developed a sense of right and wrong.

Mr Price, prosecuting counsel, told the court that Matheson, unofficially, had had a key to the boxing hall. He was thus able to come and go as he pleased, and he took Gordon Lockhart there. What, precisely, had gone on between the two before no-one knew, but Lockhart would have gone there voluntarily. It seems evident that the crucial question of stealing money from Gordon Lockhart was information given by Matheson, and was entirely without corroboration; the 'businessman' who allegedly gave it to the boy was never identified, and without Matheson's own testimony that he took it there would be no evidence of theft. Nor was any money recovered, or even proof of its existence established. 'I took the money out of his pocket. That's why I killed him. I spent the money'. Matheson, who, in the opinion of 'experts', had not developed a sense of right and wrong, alone provided the evidence required to hang him.

Matheson was duly sentenced to death, 'the only punishment provided by the law', said the Judge, adding 'the killing was one of the

MATHESON TO DIE FOR 'SORDID' MURDER

Ladies—are you going back to this?

ALBERT EDWARD MATHESON was last night sentenced to death at Durham Assizes for the murder of 15 - year - old Gordon Lockhart, of Stephenson Road, Newcastle.

An all-male jury found him guilty of capital murder, after considering their verdict for 65

Sentenced to Death ...

... but Albert Matheson did not hang.

A 'MONSTER' GOES FREE OF THE GALLOWS

By ALLAN LOFTS

ALBERT EDWARD MATHESON, a 52-year-old Newcastle labourer who was called a monster by the Lord Chief Justice, Lord Goddard, won his appeal against a murder conviction and death sentence yesterday.

Instead the Court of Criminal Appeal, who heard the case in London, substituted a verdict of manslaughter and sentenced him to 20 years imprisonment most ghoulish and sordid crimes'. But Matheson did not hang. The Court of Criminal Appeal sentenced him to 20 years imprisonment instead because the verdict of the jury was 'unreasonable'. Lord Goddard, chairing the Appeal, said 'he is a monster, there is no other word for him'. Matheson had a defence under the Homicide Act of 'diminished responsibility', which had been supported by three doctors at his trial and was not challenged. Matheson, they said, was 'suffering from such abnormality of mind as to impair substantially his mental responsibility'. He was later certified officially as 'insane' and was never released from prison.

Point to Ponder

As any experienced detective would tell you, so often it is the case that in criminal trials a court does not necessarily dispense 'justice'. In the Matheson case, the Appeal Court judges may have been correct in reducing the murder conviction to one of manslaughter on the grounds of diminished responsibility. But note also the comment that the opinion of medical experts 'was not challenged'. In other words, the sentence was liable to be reduced on a 'technicality', or the case even thrown out. Let the prosecution err in any way, no matter how trivial, and crucial evidence may be discarded and the jury, banished from the court until the judge decides on the issue, will not hear it.

'Justice' can be 'injustice'; the truth can be barred; the benefit of the doubt always lies with the accused.

Murder Without Motive

Those who would commit crime usually have a reason to do so. To steal, to gain sexual satisfaction, to exact revenge. The list is endless. The ultimate crime is no different and the reason, or 'motive', is usually vital in proving a killer's guilt. Murder is often, indeed is usually, committed by someone who knows the victim. The police seldom have to look far (although proving it in courts of law under a legal system which over-favours defendants' rights – and nowadays 'human' rights – is quite another matter). If police haven't identified a killer within 24 hours a murder will be difficult to solve.

But motive is not always apparent; nor is there always a motive at all. By any measure of human intellect, the motive for the callous slaying of Mary Ann Mackay in the middle of a city in broad daylight is impossible to fathom. It happened on a hot afternoon in Newcastle, on Monday, 18th June, 1973. Yet city shoppers, office workers and anyone passing at the time saw nothing.

She was known as Old Polly and she was 80 years of age. She had been shopping for groceries and was making her way from Gallowgate to her nearby home at St James's Terrace, which she shared with six other tenants and where she had lived for nearly forty years, of which twenty had been spent as a widow. She was 'a little old woman no-one would ever notice', but yards from her front door someone did notice. In narrow Leazes Lane, flanked by high walls, someone, for reasons best known to themselves but to date not discovered by anyone else, thrust a long-bladed knife several times through Polly's skull and left her dying on the cobblestones.

Above: Leazes Lane, scene of murder without motive.

Left: The first stage of the new East Stand at St James's Park was under construction at the time of Polly's murder.

She was found by a passer-by and taken to hospital in the belief she had fallen and cut her head. Closer examination proved otherwise. Her purse and groceries were untouched; there was no sign of interference with her person, nor indeed would it have been feasible for her attacker to have lingered to commit any sexual crime. There were no witnesses, there was no apparent motive. There was no sign of the murder weapon. Police began their enquiries with the local population, few in an area of offices, shops and bordered by a football ground and a university. Students at nearby Halls of Residents, and a nearby shelter for the homeless, visited by 'regulars' and anyone passing through was included. Few people would walk up the lane or even notice it.

The information gathered by police led to all manner of wild goose chases as detectives followed 'leads': youths seen in the area at the time, the driver of a red lorry, likely candidates from the

 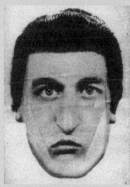 

Police identikits of a suspect in the 'Old Polly' murder. The suspect supposedly wore a leather jacket similar to this …

detached worlds of students and tramps, photofits provided by anyone who could say they saw a 'suspect'. Inevitably, anyone associated with Polly was considered suspect, like a 51-year old man who lodged at the same address and who told a newspaper that he and Polly were to be married only two days before, only for wedding plans to be 'blocked' by her family because of the difference in their ages. 'She was the greatest woman who ever lived,' he said. A romantic tale, it might have proved, but experienced detectives were bound to look deeper, and they did. The man was arrested, the man was released. As were others. And still there was no apparent motive to kill Polly. How could there be, save that of a madman?

Without motive, no manner of police questioning could succeed; unless, of course, other indisputable evidence presented itself: forensic evidence, a witness to the crime, a fingerprint, a confession. Alas, there was not a clue. The murder weapon was never discovered, no bloodstained clothing of any suspect was found. Detectives worked hard but in vain. The murder of Mary Ann Mackay remains unsolved.

SECTION SIX

THE JEALOUS SOLDIER

Holy Saviour's Church, Tynemouth.

It was around seven on a summer's eve in July. The Reverend Nichols was on his way to church, Holy Saviour's, Tynemouth, on his tricycle. As he cycled slowly, due to a broken pedal on his machine, he could not have been prepared for the sight of the two people, one, a young woman, who lay on the ground, the other a man, stooped over her, and even as he looked he saw the man striking at the woman's throat with a knife. The man ran off, leaving his victim dying on the footpath.

The victim was Mary Ann Marshall, 17 years, daughter of Robert Marshall, a 'respectable labourer' employed by Tynemouth Corporation. She had been stabbed on the left side of her neck, and her windpipe had been severed. Later, the Rev Nichols said, 'blood spurted from the wound, and her face and head and clothes were covered'. Her hands were cut in several places in her frantic attempts to ward off the knife repeatedly thrust at her by her assailant.

Others took up the chase whilst Mr Nichols attended to the victim, who had managed to get to her feet. She was leaning against the churchyard wall when Mr Nichols attended to her. He took her into the vestry, where she was unable to speak and where she died just minutes later. This was a tragic case of love, estrangement, jealousy and misguided vengeance. It ended on the scaffold at Newcastle prison, when a soldier, Samuel George Emery, was hanged for the murder of Mary Ann, or Polly, as she was known. He killed her out of jealousy. He admitted the crime; he admitted to making a ghastly mistake, for nothing of Polly's conduct could have given rise to jealousy at all.

Emery was born at West Bromwich. At 20 years of age he was a private in the South Staffordshire Regiment, which was billeted in Tynemouth Barracks. The year was 1894. Polly lived in Cross Street, Tynemouth. The two had met in the town and become sweethearts, and there had been talk of marriage. Sadly for them both, Emery was posted with his regiment to Strensall, near York. That, in those days, was as good as a million miles away to the young lovers; but the army was the army, and Emery had to go. No doubt between them they would have contrived of a way to be together again, but in the meantime they could always exchange letters. Unfortunately, one letter, from an unexpected and apparently unknown source gave Emery rise for serious concern over his sweetheart's fidelity. Its author said his Polly had been 'seeing another man'.

It is easy to say that Emery should have treated the contents of such a letter, and others received later, with caution. Why were they anonymous – if they were – and why should anyone seek to write to him about Polly, no matter what she was or wasn't up to? Someone who sought her attention, perhaps; or someone up to mischief, or acting in spite. Emery's response, born out of instant jealousy, was to write to Polly, saying 'You had better keep to yourself for I shall come when you little think of it'. His response was hardly a veiled threat.

On 21st July Emery deserted his regiment. He went to Tynemouth where he remained for two nights. On 23rd July, the day he would kill Polly, he dressed in civilian clothing, and just before 5 o'clock he went to the post office to send a telegram, but on the clerk's advice he wrote a letter, which he posted then and there, asking Polly to meet him that evening – not something that would be possible today, but the postal service was more efficient in 1894, obviously.

At the inquest, the day after Polly's murder, her father, Robert Marshall, confirmed his daughter had received a letter written on a telegram form in pencil by Emery, and contained in an envelope. 'All I saw was a sentence asking her to meet him at the place they had met the night before. I told her not to go.' 'You never saw her again?' asked the coroner. 'Not until I saw her dead body,' said Mr Marshall, weeping bitterly. He was asked if Polly had been 'keeping company' with Emery. Mr Marshall said she had. He had seen him in Tynemouth on the Saturday evening and was aware that he and Polly had been together on Saturday and Sunday, and that he (Emery) was in the Marshall house on the Sunday, when Emery had worn civilian clothes. He said Emery and his daughter had wanted to get married, but they were too young to do so without consent, which had not been given. What's more, Mr Marshall, himself a former soldier, objected to Polly meeting Emery that weekend because he knew he was due to report to camp by 10 p.m.

Thomas Moar, ironmonger, told the court Emery had called at his shop about 4.30 on Monday afternoon. He had been shown a case of knives, all of which Emery had rejected. 'None of them is large enough,' he said. So Mr Moar showed him the largest he had, a clasp knife. Emery asked Moar to sharpen it on an oil stone, which was done, and Emery bought it.

That Monday evening Polly and Emery met in Percy Park and strolled to the church, she probably delighted to see him, he with murder in mind. We can never know what was said, but witnesses would say that at one point she placed her arms around his neck, suggesting perhaps she believed all was well. But all was not well. As the Reverend Nichols testified, as he approached Holy Saviour's on his tricycle the two persons he saw struggling on the ground were 'like two boys playing'. He saw the young man strike his victim two or three times, then jump up, at which point he saw him 'full face'. The man was wearing a light cap and brown suit. He ran off along the path at the back of the church. In the coroner's court, he said the prisoner, Emery, was the man 'to the best of my belief', but could not say so absolutely.

At least two men gave chase. One was Edward Stacey, a railway clerk, who was passing with his mother. He saw Polly's head hanging over the kerbstone as her assailant struck at her. The man ran off through the wicket gate and disappeared somewhere behind the railway station. Another was James Gibson, a chemist, who encountered a woman who called out to him to 'stop that man'. Gibson caught up with Emery, who stopped and faced Mr Gibson, flashing the knife before his face. 'He had the appearance of a madly desperate man,' said Gibson. Emery ran off again, pursued by Gibson. He chased

Formerly the House of Correction, North Shields. Samuel Emery was arrested nearby – convenient for his subsequent incarceration inside.

him over a wall, across a field and through a garden, after which, exhausted, he lost him in the railway sidings.

After making his escape, Emery disappeared for an hour or so until, as darkness came, he turned up at the Crescent Tavern, Hudson Street, where, not surprisingly, everyone was talking about the murder. Emery was curious. 'Is she dead?' he asked. When told she was, he said, 'I saw the murder. A soldier did it. I am a soldier myself.' Emery, it seems, had the murder on his conscience. It was as though he wanted to tell someone – and he did. He asked the landlady to give him paper, pen and ink. When she did, he wrote something, which he sealed in the envelope and handed to her, telling her not to open it until he had been gone for five minutes. Emery had written a confession.

At 11.35 that night Inspector Alexander McKenzie and Sergeant Henry McQueen, on foot patrol, met Samuel Emery near the House of Correction in Tynemouth Road. Emery matched the description of the killer, and held the open knife in his hand. Insp McKenzie said to him, 'I charge you with murdering Mary Ann Marshall.' When told she was dead, Emery replied, 'Thank God for that. I would like to see her dead.' At the police station came another confession, this time of a more official nature. 'I came from Strensall Camp near York with the intention of murdering Mary Ann Marshall, on the 21st July 1894. I delayed it until the 23rd. I wrote a note asking her to meet me beside Holy Saviour's Church. I met her about 6.10 p.m. We went for a walk through the fields, past a farmhouse, where we sat down until 8.10. I was quite sober when I committed the deed about half past eight'.

In November, Emery stood trial before Justice Charles at Newcastle. That he had killed Polly was not in doubt. But Mr Blake, defending, said that even though Emery called himself a murderer, it was for the jury, not he, to decide whether he was or was not. He invited them to return a manslaughter verdict instead, or at least recommend mercy if they found him guilty of murder. Murder it was, with no recommendation. The judge, passing sentence, said, 'I earnestly beg you to repent to the crime and seek pardon and mercy from Almighty God.' Emery picked up his cap and went to the cells.

Clearly with thoughts of 'insanity' in mind, albeit after his trial and conviction, Emery was examined by Dr Nicholson, of Broadmoor Criminal Lunatic Asylum. But there would be no reprieve. On 11th December he went to the scaffold at Newcastle Prison. He was reported to show a 'penitent demeanour', and displayed no fear. His last words to the prison chaplain were, 'Pray for the poor girl whose life I have taken'. He never disclosed the identity of the person who wrote to him about Polly.

Unusually, the press were not permitted to witness the execution so they wrote instead of events outside the prison. The crowd, it was reported, gathered before daylight, with groups forming on the higher

Set in stone. Mary Marshall's initials and a heart can be seen today, carved in the stonework of the churchyard wall.

ground at the top of Worswick Street. They were working men and women, and their children. 'The men and women smoked, and children listened with ears pricked and keen eyes …' There being no element of doubt as to the guilt of the culprit – often the main talking point at hangings – they discussed the issue of capital punishment itself. Many expressed sympathy for Emery, possibly based on his mental state rather than his deed on the fateful day.

The memory of this tragic tale is perpetuated by the weathered initials of Mary Marshall, and a heart, chiselled into a coping stone on top of the wall of Holy Saviour's Church the site of her murder. Passers-by, and those who wait in the nearby bus shelter on the Broadway, will not readily see the inscription, a reminder of a tragic and, sadly, determined act of jealously.

Point to Ponder

Those who would advocate capital punishment as a deterrent to other would-be killers would do well to consider the facts of this case. Samuel Emery clearly planned his mission of murder: he deserted his army post, travelled to Tynemouth where, two days later, with ample to time to change his mind about killing an innocent young woman, he obtained civilian clothing and a knife, then met with Mary Ann Marshall and after walking with her to the church he stabbed her to death, a crime as ruthless as it was premeditated. He would have known the consequences. Yet, motivated by jealousy, he carried out the deed. Hanging did not deter him at all.

Justice On The Moor

The North East was well served with suitable venues to hang murderers and other felons, Newgate and, later, Carliol Prison, Newcastle, and Durham being the most prevalent. Before the public were barred from witnessing the ultimate penalty for the ultimate crime, you could see justice being done on Newcastle's Town Moor, that vast expanse of land so jealously guarded against incursion by those who would build on or otherwise develop it.

Charles Smith was hanged on the Moor, in 1817. A Sunderland man, he had served in the army and worked at Fulwell Lime Works. His crime, to which he did not confess, was the murder of Charles Stewart, the 'keeper' of Ouseburn Pottery, who was 'cruelly beaten and bruised on the head and different parts of his body by two persons'. It happened on 4th December, 1816, when the said two persons, having thus assaulted Mr Stewart, tied his legs together, bound his head so as to suffocate him and left him for dead before ransacking the premises. The next morning, when Mr Stewart was found, still alive, he named Charles Smith as one of the men who 'had so ill-treated him'; he had recognised him, he said, 'not only by his figure, but by his voice, as he spoke with a broad Irish accent'. He was unable to identify the second man. He died three weeks later in the infirmary of his wounds and then, and only then, were 'officers dispatched to arrest Smith'.

They found in his house a large, bloodstained oaken flick (bludgeon); his breeches, one of his boots and a stocking were also bloodstained. These items were the strongest evidence against him, stronger even than Stewart's identification, it seems. Smith protested his innocence, but was condemned to death. He was reported to be depressed; who wouldn't have been?

The judge, evidently concerned about the 'informality' in the

---

THE LAST

DYING WORDS. SPEECH. AND CONFESSION,

OF

CHARLES SMITH,

Who was executed on NEWCASTLE TOWN MOOR, December 3d, 1817, for the Murder of

CHARLES STEWART, at the OUSEBURN POTTERY, near Newcastle.

I, CHARLES SMITH, do solemnly declare before Almighty God, at whose tribunal I must shortly appear, and in whose presence I shall stand acquitted of the Murder of CHARLES STEWART, for whom I must suffer an ignominious death in this world; but I die in the firm belief of seeing God in mercy, through frain from taking notice of the particulars pointed out in the wretched man's confession. The first a wanton and foolish waste of the hard earned pittance, destined by Providence for the maintenance of his family;—the second, a stupid refraining, and absenting himself from the observance of God's holy ordinances.

Charles Smith's 'confession'.

evidence of the deceased man, Mr Stewart, wanted the case referred on a point of law to twelve judges. Smith, meanwhile, signed a 'confession', meaning he was innocent of murder, saying that he 'freely forgave all his enemies and those who had sworn falsely against him'. It was not a confession to the crime. 'Never in my whole life,' said Smith, 'did the crime of murder ever enter into my head, and no person can charge me with any crime other than foolishly mis-spending my earnings and neglecting attendance on the ordinances of God. I solemnly declare before God, on whose mercy I rely and before whom I shall soon appear, that I never knocked down Charles Stewart, or tied his feet, or shed his blood, which has been falsely sworn against me. I hope no person will be so base as to upbraid my dear wife and children with the murder for which I am now going to suffer ...'

The Lord Chief Justice had taken ill, which had somehow prevented the judges from considering the point of law on the case. However, on 3rd December, 1817, the warrant of execution was signed, one day short of one year exactly since the crime. The warrant was read over to Smith, who was asked to name his accomplice. He said he had nothing more to say, except that he requested his body might be given to his dear wife immediately after his execution. Alas, this was not possible. He was placed on a cart and taken to the gallows they had erected on the Moor. 'Officers of police and a vast concourse of people joined the procession', and after the usual words of religious expression Smith was 'launched into the arms of death'.

Print depicting the hanging of Charles Smith on Newcastle Town Moor. Public hangings were very popular occasions.

THE DEATH PENALTY:
HANGING AND HANGMEN

'Prisoner X, you are sentenced to be taken hence to the prison in which you were last confined, and from there to a place of execution where you will be hanged by the neck until dead, and thereafter your body buried within the precincts of the prison. And may the Lord have mercy upon your soul.'

So said the judge at the Courts of Assize in passing sentence on a person condemned to death for a 'capital' crime, as murder was in England and Wales until 1965. Indeed it was the only sentence for murder, as life imprisonment is today. There are those who believe hanging to be a barbarous means of judiciously taking life (as well as believing any form of execution to be wrong), yet, in the United Kingdom, as far as humanely taking the life of a person was concerned, the authorities had just about 'got hanging right' by the time they abolished it. It wasn't always so.

Newcastle Magazine Gate. A former gateway to the city, near where the Swing Bridge stands today. The heads of those executed were displayed in gruesome fashion as a reminder to those who would transgress the law.

'Drawing, hanging and quartering', often misquoted, dates back to at least the 13th century. The condemned man (never a woman) was drawn to the place of execution on a hurdle, a fence-like apparatus pulled by a horse. Then he was hanged without a 'drop', i.e. strung up to slowly strangle. And then, still alive and conscious, he was cut down to have his genitals cut off, his intestines and other organs removed and burned before his eyes, and finally his head removed and his body cut up, or quartered. Such was the fate of Guy Fawkes, in 1606. He wasn't burned, as his effigy is today!

Women were burned at the stake, as it was considered indecent to reveal naked female flesh. Or, if they were lucky, they were hanged in the centre of the pyre just before it was lit to spare them the agony of the flames. The last woman to die by this method was Christian Murphy, who, in 1789 was marched past the hanging bodies of her eight male co-defendants at Newgate, London (including her husband) and put to death for coining offences.

Hanging was an ancient, and for many years, an accepted form of punishment. Around 1500, as well as for murder you'd hang for treason, petty treason (murdering a husband or wife, master or servant), robbery, larceny (theft), rape and arson. In 1699 they added 'shoplifting to the value of five shillings'. You'd get a police caution now. How times have changed.

In the18th century, the authorities found a new way to deal with transgressors of the law: transportation. You could be sent to the colonies for stealing a rabbit to feed a starving family. This was replaced by 'penal servitude'. Gradually, the number of capital crimes was reduced; by 1861 you could hang for murder, treason, mutiny and piracy. They hanged you in public, but an Act of Parliament forbade this from 1868. The last person to hang in this country for treason was William Joyce, 'Lord Haw-Haw', who broadcast Nazi propaganda to Britain during the war.

Things started to change after the Homicide Act, 1957, when hanging for murder was only possible in certain circumstances. There can be no doubt this was not the wish of the public, and still isn't; rather it was the will of their elected politicians. The conditions were:

> Murder committed in the course or furtherance of theft;
> Murder by shooting or explosion;
> Murder whilst resisting arrest or escape;
> Murder of a police or prison officer;
> Two murders committed on separate occasions.

Thus, if you stabbed someone to death you could not be executed, but if you shot them dead you would be. If you raped and murdered a woman you could not be executed, but if you murdered her to steal her shopping you would hang.

Today, hanging is still the secondmost popular form of execution worldwide, after shooting. In this country, it continued until 1965.

In 1964 two men who murdered a man at Workington, Cumbria, were hanged at the same time in different locations; they were the last to hang in the U.K. The last woman to hang in England was Ruth Ellis, in 1955, for the murder of her lover. In 1965 capital punishment was suspended, and abolished altogether in 1969 (except for treason and piracy, but they too were effectively abolished). In 1998 the authority of elected politicians in the U.K. was also abolished, when power was ceded to the European Union 'Human Rights' laws.

Many of the subjects of this book were hanged, at different times but always for the same reason: murder. And, as hanging may not be quite as straightforward as it appears, we can look at some of the grisly details ...

Hanging without a 'drop' causes slow strangulation as the noose tightens under the hanged person's bodyweight. The jugular vein and carotid arteries become constricted, and the windpipe is closed. Usually the person hanging will struggle, a natural reaction to events, but death is usually quite quick and always inevitable as the face turns blue and the tongue often protrudes. There may be effusions of urine and faeces; men can have erections and even ejaculate. Sometimes a short 'drop' of a few inches was made, but this would neither break the neck nor lessen pain.

Newgate Prison, Newcastle – the north front. Another former gateway to the city. Conditions inside must have been grim. It was demolished in the 1820s.

NEWCASTLE UPON TYNE. Gaoler, *John Gale.* He is a tallow-chandler, and lives near the prison. Salary 100l. Fees, felons 14s. 4d.; debtors 14s. 4d.; besides which the Under-sheriff demands 2s. 6d. on discharge of a writ from the Court of King's Bench or Common Pleas.

Chaplains, the Rev. Mr. Moifer and the Rev. Mr. Perkins. Duty, on Sunday none; but on Wednesday and Friday prayers; and once a month a sermon. The chaplains officiate alternately a month each. Salary, 10l. the corporation, and 10l. Sir *Walter Blacket.* Surgeon, Mr. *William Fife.* Salary, none. He makes a bill, which is allowed by the magistrates in sessions. Allowance, debtors, two pence a day, on petition; but this the turnkey told me was very difficult to obtain. Allowance to felons three pence a-day. Number of prisoners Feb. 7, 1802, debtors 13, felons, &c. 12.

This prison is the Gate at the upper end of the town, and was formerly a fortified gateway. There is no court; but one might be made of the vacant ground that lies West of the gaol, at a little expence, as the town wall is one side of it. At my visit, there was a pig-stye, with pigs, ducks, &c. in it. On the right-hand side of the gateway there is a passage, eight yards by two yards and a half, in which there is a cock to supply this part of the prison with water; and adjoining to this is the condemned-room, the only one upon the ground floor; all the others are up stairs, both clean and airy. It is about six yards by four yards and a half, with a fire-place and an iron-grated window, which looks to the street; but, to prevent conversation with passengers, or files, &c. being conveyed to them, there is a palisaded wall erected at a little distance from the felons window. It is called the *Cap Room.* There are four rooms in the felons gaol; and no prisoners here have fetters, unless they be riotous.

Over the condemned-room is another, the same size, which looks to the street. There is a small court, 54 feet by 17, with a bathing-tub in it; but, not being secure, the felons have not the use of it. The left side of the gateway is the gaol for debtors; and on the staircase leading to their apartments there is framed and glazed, " Friends visiting the debtors in this prison are to take notice, that the following are the

hours of admission, which cannot be departed from, except on very particular occasions: from eight to nine in the morning; from twelve to one at noon; from four to five in the evening. Those who neglect to come out at the appointed hour must remain till the next opening."

Debtors have no court, but walk on the battery at the top of the gaol, which is nearly 34 feet square, with a flagged floor, and a sewer in one corner; and on the flat leads, about 40 feet square. To these two places they have access at all times, from morning till night. There is no distinction of debtors. The corporation allows an iron bedstead, a bed-tick, which is filled with new chaff every three months, one under blanket, two upper blankets, and two coverlets (which are scoured every three months), both to debtors, felons, and all descriptions of prisoners. There are eight lodging-rooms for debtors; and every one sleeps single if the prison will admit it. They succeed to the best rooms by seniority of confinement; and every one is required to attend Divine service (except prevented by illness), who does not profess himself of a different persuasion. All prisoners are allowed as much firing as they can consume without waste, and mops, brooms, pails, &c. to keep the prison clean. Any one who misbehaves is tried by a court, at which the senior debtor presides, and fined according to rules laid down for preserving good behaviour in the prison. All communication with him is interdicted till the fine is paid. If he conceives himself hardly judged, he applies to the keeper, who examines into the matter, and settles it accordingly. This relates to petty offences committed against the peace of the prison.

This is one of the very few gaols that have what is called in London the *Rules.* They extend South of the prison to a running water, arched over, called Execution Dock, and on the East of the prison, down High Fryer-street about 200 yards, to a rivulet called Lork Burn *, now arched over with

---

* Lork Burn, up which for a considerable way the tide flowed formerly, made a division antiently in the lower part of the *Side,* a street so called. This runner of water was covered over with stone A.D. 1696. Vide Hutchinson's History of Durham.

stone.

1806: a Mr Neild visited Newgate Prison …

Typically no 'drop' hangings occurred when the prisoner stood on a cart and was taken to the place of execution, a rope placed around his neck and the cart simply moved forward leaving him to hang. In the old 'Wild West', baddies would sit astride a horse, then the rope was thrown over a suitable branch of a tree and the horse given a wallop, leaving him to hang by strangulation.

Newcastle Prison, 1828. It replaced the old Newgate
Gaol.

'Standard drop hanging' meant a drop of about five feet or so,
through a trapdoor. This would cause considerable damage to neck
muscles, without breaking the neck, so that the person hanged suffered
as much if not more than with no drop. The 'long drop', used in Britain
after 1874, was the most humane form of hanging. It was introduced
by William Marwood, a cobbler, who didn't hang anyone until he was
over 50. The advantage (if it may be deemed so) of the long drop was
that the prisoner's neck was broken and unconsciousness was instant
when he (or she) had fallen a pre-determined distance, calculated by a
formula taking into account the prisoner's body weight. It was so
precise the Home Office determined the 'length of drop' for persons of
certain weights. Getting the drop right was important: too short and the
neck would not break, causing great agony and distress to the prisoner,
too long and his head might come off.

Cause of death by the long drop method is still strangulation, but because the head snaps instantly backwards and ruptures the spinal cord, the prisoner becomes unconscious immediately and does not suffer pain (not that anyone hanged by this method lived to say so). Death follows quickly, although in all cases the body is left hanging for an hour to be certain. As well as 'benefiting' the person being hanged, at least as far as physical suffering is concerned, the long drop saved those involved in the hanging process much trauma. Then again, there are those who would argue physical pain for murderers is no bad thing.

Some hangmen became famous, notably (in chronological order): William Calcraft, the longest serving hangman who applied the short drop method (his 'clients' suffered ghastly deaths as a result), the aforementioned William Marwood, James Berry, who tried and failed to hang John Lee on gallows that worked perfectly well when three times tested but whose trapdoor would on no account open when Lee stood on it (the prison governor called it off and Lee was pardoned), and still with Berry when he hanged Robert Goodale whose head came off because the drop was too long (he weighed 15 stones), and three others who slowly strangled to death because the drop was too short, and a woman of the same surname, Berry, to whom he was not related but had danced with at a police ball; James Billington and his sons, Thomas, William and John, Henry Pierrepoint, John Ellis, the hanging barber who wrote his memoirs then committed suicide, Thomas Pierrepoint (Henry's brother), and Albert Pierrepoint (Thomas's nephew), who hanged around 450 people in the 20th century.

Point to Ponder

One man who survived the noose was John Smith, hanged at Tyburn in 1705. After the cart that carried him was taken away he hung for quarter of an hour when the crowd called 'reprieve'. (It was Christmas.) After being cut down he recovered, and had this to say about his experience:

'I was for some time sensible of great pain, occasioned by the weight of my body, and felt my spirits in great commotion, violently pressing upwards. I saw a great blaze of glaring light that seemed to go out of my eyes in a flash, and I lost all sense of pain. After I was cut down I began to come to myself and the blood and spirits forcing themselves into their former channels put me into such intolerable pain I could have wished those hanged who cut me down.'

Now we know.

Botched: The Hangings That Went Wrong

William Marwood might claim credit for the introduction of the 'measured drop' into the hanging procedure, yet he was responsible for a botched hanging at Durham. The man who suffered was 33-year old James Burton, who murdered his wife at Silksworth, in 1883. They were parted, and one night Burton chased her across a railway and up an embankment where he bashed her head in with a blunt instrument, then buried her in a ditch under some stones. After trying to commit suicide, first by an overdose of laudanum and then trying to hang himself, he ended up on the gallows.

When the bolt was drawn Burton should have plummeted to instant doom. Instead, still alive, he swung to and fro, and when Marwood hauled his writhing form upward he discovered the rope had got caught up under Burton's arm and the noose had moved up over his chin. So he replaced the rope and pushed him back down into the pit. Burton took some time to die.

Not that 'botched hangings' were unusual, as the case of Matthew Atkinson proves. Drunk after a day's drinking and shooting, Atkinson returned home one night to find no meal ready and no fire in the grate. This was not good enough for a Winlaton coal miner, who chased his wife to a neighbour's house where he beat her to death with his fists, a poker and other implements.

Durham. The site of many an execution. The splendid Cathedral and Castle tower over today's top security prison.

Those who knew the couple, whilst not condoning murder, had some sympathy with Atkinson as it was known his wife consorted with several local males, particularly when her husband was at work. Sentenced to death on 16th March, 1865, at Durham, a large crowd turned up to watch Atkinson hang. By then public executions were only 'half seen'; whilst spectators could see the hangman place the hood over the doomed man's head and the noose around his neck, the drop was screened, so that he disappeared from sight once the trapdoor opened. So it was with Atkinson, except that his disappearance was followed by the sound of a thud as he hit the ground. The rope had snapped.

Feelings of sympathy now turned to concern that Atkinson might be hurt! The crowd cheered when he appeared none the worse for wear and waited in uncertainty until a thicker rope was found. Clearly the first 'drop' had been too long, and a shorter one was arranged as once more Matthew Atkinson climbed the scaffold. Down he went to an agonising death, as this time the drop was too short, leaving him to slowly strangle. Those watching the jerking rope as Atkinson struggled out of sight were not pleased.

Then there was the ghastly execution of Ewan Macdonald. For this we go back to the massacre of Bonnie Prince Charlie's Jacobite army at Culloden in 1746, and afterwards, when Scots soldiers, still resenting the 'auld enemy', found themselves serving King and country in England. So it was one March night in 1752 a party of soldiers of the Royal Highlanders found themselves in a tavern in Newcastle's Bigg Market, a place of heavy drinking and bawdy fighting (has anything changed?).

It seems the Tyneside locals made fun of Macdonald's kilt. No doubt Macdonald, a strapping fellow who could put himself about – you can imagine the scene already – put up with this for a while until, inevitably, he reacted by giving a man called Parker a dig in the ribs. Parker ran outside, pursued by Macdonald. Then Parker's younger brother, Robert, got involved, and the enraged Macdonald stabbed him in the throat before returning to the tavern where he set about anyone he could lay his hands on. A group of soldiers dragged Macdonald away, and he was committed to the Assizes where he was sentenced to hang. Hang him they did, but not before he tried to throw the hangman from the scaffold! After an hour they cut him down and took him to Surgeon's Hall for dissection. As the body lay on the slab the surgeons were called away, and on their return they found Macdonald sitting up rubbing a sore neck.

He begged for his life, but one of surgeons picked up a mallet and with Macdonald fighting desperately he was clubbed to death. An amazing sequel to the story followed, when the surgeon who so mercilessly dispatched him was found dead in his stables with head injuries, presumably kicked to death by his horse. Or, as the locals believed, by Macdonald's ghost, wreaking an exact revenge.

Copy of a signed confession by one Patrick Forbes, who admitted he was 'very drunk and not conscious to myself of having done anything to cause the death of my dear wife'. He 'begged pardon to all persons whom I have injured and forgave all who had offended me'. His written confession is dated 23rd August 1850. He was hanged the following day. (Original document held in Newcastle Archives)

VIGILANTES' NIGHTMARE

John Patterson, murdered by Joseph William Noble, was buried at St Albans Church, Windy Nook.

'The criminal annals of the north country have not for some years produced a case which has aroused so much public interest. A midnight vigil, the appearance of a man wearing a false beard, the dramatic production of a revolver – and murder!' So reported the *Newcastle Journal* at the beginning of the trial of Joseph William Noble, 45, at Durham Assizes in March, 1908. Noble declared himself 'not guilty'. The issue was straightforward enough, as counsel for the prosecution explained: was Noble a killer, and, if so, had he committed murder or manslaughter when he shot and killed John Patterson in the Windy Nook Co-op, Gateshead, the previous November?

It all started so innocuously. Three times over three weeks someone had picked the lock at the butchers shop on the corner of Union Street and Harwood Street, and stolen meat in such small quantity that its disappearance would have gone unnoticed except the books didn't balance. No money had been taken, no damage had been caused. But shopbreaking, as it was then, was a crime nonetheless and something had to be done. So it was on Thursday, 1st November, 1907, four men began an overnight vigil in the Co-op. John Patterson, Christopher Carr and George Ather, all employed at a nearby quarry, and butcher's apprentice Joseph Cowell, secreted themselves in the office and butchery department and waited. A string was attached to an 'incandescent light' which, when pulled, would illuminate the shop, revealing the identity of the intruder.

One can picture the scene that dark night. There would be no traffic in those days, no activity on the streets outside. Just silence and darkness as they awaited the intruder who might or might not keep an unexpected appointment with our vigilantes. Equally, one can imagine racing heartbeats when, just after one o'clock, someone was heard at the door and a light was seen. But it was only the local constable, PC Thompson, doing his round. The vigil continued until 4.10 a.m., when the street light outside unexpectedly went out …

Moments later there was the sound of a key turning the lock, then the faint sight of a figure crouching in the open doorway. He held a lamp in his left hand as he moved slowly into the shop, revealing a beard and moustache. He wore a dark coat and carried a stick under his arm. He moved first into the 'killing' house, then back into the middle of the shop where, next to the hanging carcases of two pigs, Patterson, Carr and Ather sprang upon him as young Cowell pulled the string and turned on the light. According to later testimony, the man 'fought like a tiger.' As they struggled desperately on the floor Carr picked up a butcher's steel (a knife sharpener) and struck the intruder two or three hard blows on the head. At this point the man was pinned down, captured surely, but Ather, believing Carr had used too much force, pleaded, 'For God's sake, don't use the man so.' The intruder concurred, saying, 'You are behaving badly to me.' Around which point his moustache and whiskers fell off.

Carr, having been rebuked, released hold, whereupon the intruder reached into his pocket and drew a revolver. At once he shot Patterson in the head, then Carr in the top of a leg. Stunned, the men backed off. The man ran into another room, climbed up to a window and, kicking out the glass, dropped into the street to make his escape. As he lowered himself from the window, he was challenged by Ather, who had run around the corner and now struck him on the leg with a hammer. The man fled, but he wasn't yet quite clear of apprehension, nor indeed serious injury, for Ather's wife, alerted by the noise and having heard the shots, had risen from her bed and still in her nightie and wielding an axe now chased him up the dark street, alas to no avail as he fled from sight. Brave woman she, and just as well he escaped, you might think, bearing in mind he still carried the gun and had just shot two people.

And, sadly, had murdered one, for John Patterson, 33, a family man with twins, a boy and a girl, died on his way to hospital two hours later. The post mortem examination would reveal that the bullet had penetrated his left eyebrow and lodged in his brain. But was there a second man? Terrified, John Joseph Cowell, the apprentice butcher, fled the moment he saw Patterson shot – only to find another man in the doorway. He didn't hang around to enquire of his identity, but went for PC Thompson.

At the scene, police recovered the intruder's false moustache and beard, the hazel stick he had carried and took a plaster cast of a smooth footprint, believed to have been made by someone wearing rubber galoshes. At daylight, PC Thompson traced footprints leading from the shop and around the top of the quarry, the intruder's escape route possibly. The 'second man' who had startled Cowell turned out to be Robert Carter, a 'knocker up', whose job it was to knock workmen from their beds. He must have been as surprised as Cowell when he came upon the commotion at the shop. It is as well the intruder did not make his escape through the door as Carter appeared, or he might have shot him too.

THE NEWCASTLE DAILY JOURNAL, FRIDAY, NOVEMBER 29, 1907.

S IN MOROCCO.

nts from Algiers.

RS' FIGHTING.

ich Losses.

r's Telegrams.)
Paris, Thursday.
" publishes the following tele-
nforcements, including artillery,
rom Algiers. The natives who
tier to put themselves under
that the Beni Snassen and Riff
into a compact to attack the
e an attempt to capture Ujda,
Marnia. Uneasiness prevails in
the authorities of Port Say and
for ships to be sent to take away

WINDY NOOK TRAGEDY.

Inquest at Felling.

VERDICT OF WILFUL MURDER
AGAINST NOBLE.

Wholesale Seizures in Prisoner's
House.

IMPORTANT FRESH EVIDENCE.

Yesterday, the inquest respecting the death of John Patterson, who was killed by a revolver shot at Windy Nook Co-operative Store early on the morning of the 1st inst., was resumed at Felling Police Station, and

value of these is estimated at about £10. They not been reported to him as missing. Superintendent Hemby said witness had not id fied one quarter of the whole property seized by police at Noble's house.

Melville, in reply to the jury, said he identifie articles.

NOBLE'S PREVIOUS CONDUCT.
Thos. Y. Nicholson, a gardener in the emp Mr John Simpson, High Heworth, said he had the accused man Noble for eight or nine year had seen Noble sometimes about six or seven on Sunday morning. About twelve months met him one morning in Leam Drive wearing beard. Witness said to him: "I know you Noble smiled and made no reply. He was we coat similar to the one produced.

ARREST AND IDENTIFICATION OF N
Inspector McDonald said on the 4th Nove company with P.C. Nesbit, he went to the P Works of the North-Eastern Railway. N sent for, and came to the time office. Witn "I won't waste any words, but ask you to your cap, and let me examine your head took off his cap. Witness examined his found two wounds on the back of the he were recent wounds. Witness said: "Ho get the injuries to your head? He answer the injury last Tuesday. I was taking a

'Desperate Affair at Windy Nook.'

75

Four days later police had a man in custody. Joseph William Noble, 50, a blacksmith of the North East Railway Company, was arrested soon after arriving at work at 6 a.m. He lived at Store Street, less than five minutes' walk from the scene of the crime. He was married 'with two or three children', and known to be a quiet, morose character who scarcely spoke to his workmates; he had worked for the company for over 10 years and was a good timekeeper. Noble started work at six each morning, as he had done on Friday, just two hours after the shootings. When asked to remove his cap police found he had recent injuries to his head. When asked to roll up a trouser leg he did so only a little way until persuaded otherwise, when bruising consistent with being struck by a hammer was revealed.

How police identified Noble isn't known exactly, except that with local knowledge they might have good cause to suspect him. But it should be clear that between them Ather, Carr and Cowell did not name Noble before he was arrested, although they all knew him. It was only later, at the police court, that Ather said he had 'formed the opinion that the man was Noble'. Carr, who had known him for years, didn't name him until he had been arrested, although, as he explained later at the trial, 'I was too frightened of him. I only spoke to him once when he was going to knock my head off'. Cowell said he had known Noble for seven years but had not recognised him in the shop. The day after his arrest, Ather and Cowell identified Joe Noble at Felling police station. Little wonder they did!

At Noble's home police discovered, among other things, a bunch of skeleton keys and a box of 48 cartridges, gun barrels, a jemmy, some hazel sticks, similar to the one the intruder carried, and a coat in a tub half-full of water, placed there to dissolve blood stains, perhaps. The bullets recovered from Patterson and Carr were .32 in. calibre, and both had been discharged from cartridge cases similar to at least two such cases found at Noble's house.

The case against Noble gained momentum. John Stoker, a coal miner, said on 1st November, the morning of the murder, on his way home from work, he passed Joe Noble on the street (this was in the middle of the night). 30-40 minutes later he heard shots and the sound of breaking glass. He went to Union Street where he saw a man's legs dangling from the window of the boiler house of the Co-op, and another man strike them with a hammer. Around 5.30 a.m., Matthew Kay saw Noble going to work. This would mean Noble, after shooting Patterson and Carr about 4.20 a.m. and being struck on the head with a butcher's steel and hit on the leg with a hammer and then escaping from the axe-wielding Mrs Athey, must have got home shortly after and about an hour later gone to work.

James Melville, the manager at the Co-op, was shown a quantity of clothing found at Noble's home by the police. In all, 120 items were identified by their markings. None was listed as 'missing' but neither had Noble bought them. Stolen along with meat on his nocturnal visits is the supposition. Thomas Nicholson, a gardener, told police that 12 months before he'd seen Noble out and about sporting a false beard. 'I know you, Joe,' Nicholson had said, to which Noble had merely smiled. Noble would say Nicholson was mistaken.

When Noble stood trial for his life he appeared confident and composed. Was he a killer? Had he deliberately shot Patterson either with the intent to kill him, or recklessly? Or, as defence counsel suggested, if he was the killer, had he fired his gun in self defence? After all, even though he was a shopbreaker, he must have feared for his life, especially when struck over the head several times by a butcher's steel. The evidence was strong, but not without fault.

Ather knew Noble. Yet even after the intruder's hat and whiskers had come off, and he was illuminated in the shop light, Athey had said. '… don't use the man so', as opposed to 'Joe' or similar. He had not recognised him. And he admitted he had seen Noble's name in the newspaper before 'identifying' him at the police station. On the murder vs manslaughter issue, Carr said, 'The man shot John Patterson deliberately. Then he shot me …'. Then he added, 'I said to myself 'It is Joe Noble?' Why didn't he tell the police his name? Because he was afraid of the man who would 'knock his head off'?

None of the witnesses had mentioned Noble's name before being told it was he who was in custody; Carr even expressed the view that the man was not Joe Noble. Maybe they were all afraid of the hard-man blacksmith. As with so many cases, identification evidence seemed flawed. Referring to the street light, which had been extinguished just before the intruder entered the shop, Inspector Lambert said he was able to turn off the light with the recovered hazel stick, and Noble had several such sticks at home. Of Noble's clothing, Mr Stock, the County Analyst, said there were bloodstains on a vest, and greasy smears on the back of a coat similar to that of a hog's – meaning it could have brushed against the hanging pigs' carcases.

Noble said he owned gun barrels and cartridges because he repaired guns, and produced billheads to support this. He said he went shooting and kept ferrets. The jemmy had belonged to his father, and as a blacksmith he used a jemmy legitimately. The hazel sticks were used to build nets to catch sparrows. His head wounds he had sustained at work when he was removing an iron bar and 'three or four' others had struck him; the bruising to his leg was down to bumping into a wheelbarrow. Such injuries should have been reported as a matter of company policy. They had not been, but then maybe a man like Joe Noble would not bother. The false whiskers he dismissed as a 'story', which would mean Thomas Nicholson was lying. At the time of the killing, Noble said he was at home. Curiously, there appears to be no recorded testimony of his wife to corroborate this. He denied owning a revolver.

The jury, in deciding whether Noble was the killer and whether, if he was, he had committed murder or manslaughter, took 45 minutes to find him guilty of murder. Noble's confidence now deserted him as he clutched the iron rail of the dock. 'I am innocent', he said. Donning the back cap, the judge asked him if he had anything else to say. 'You might break my neck,' said Noble, 'but I don't think you will break my heart'. He was hanged at Durham on 24th March, 1908.

— THE NEWCASTLE DAILY JOURNAL, WEDNESDAY, MARCH 4, 1908.

WINDY NOOK TRAGEDY.

:o:

NOBLE GUILTY AND SENTENCED TO DEATH.

The Prisoner's Defiance.

BURGLAR'S TOOLS, INJURIES, AND EXPLANATION.

After a trial lasting two days Joseph William Noble, blacksmith, was, at Durham Winter Assizes yesterday, found guilty of the murder of John Patterson, within Windy Nook Co-operative Store, early on the morning of 1st November last. The case has excited great interest throughout the country owing to all the circumstances connected with the tragedy being of a somewhat unusual character.

That murder should have been committed over petty thefts of meat seems the strangest part of the story, and that three men holding responsible positions as part of the executive committee of a

[left column, partially legible] uld have a new naval base in the ment had decided to proceed with atter of fact, they were not going have to go to work, and it would m of money. (Hear, hear.) LESS FINANCE. AMBERLAIN expressed himself Sir Charles Dilke as to increased in the future, and having regard considered the boast of the First y that the vote for new construc- e lowest on record, convicted the less finance, and an evasion of Opposition cheers.) To dawdle e contemplated at Rosyth was calculated that at least £2,400,000 ure would fall upon their estimates t increase would be repeated in year following. The Govern- a system of deferred payments. was not a system of living on position had a right to protest burdens being consciously and on future years, while present ed and scraped away in order ancial needs of the Government, resent this year a more favour- y had any real right to lay Opposition cheers.) ssed for a fuller statement from iralty on the subject of small provided in adequate numbers, were to perform their work in said, still curiosity on this sub- was changing to suspicion and

[right column, partially legible] own, but he had repaired one or two. H that time any to repair. The two empty o were used for measuring shots to fill oth need to go to work by train from Felling He very often had bacon for his breakfa THE WOUNDS ON THE PRIS As to the cuts on his head, they were ge morning, October 29th. He went up for and taking up the bar three or four s struck the back of his head. The bars w twelve feet long, and a beam prevente them out easily. He was to make st iron. He took the iron bar with a pair while at the steam hammer the tongs the body. As to the mark on the leg, against a barrow in the dark at his Little accidents of this kind were usu He had heard Nicholson's story o down the road with false whiskers. truth in that. He had never had a produced. He had also never put an front of his house. As to the grease spots, it could ea throwing his coat down on to the wife had been cooking with lard, pork rents in his trousers were caused by of iron that he was bundling up. He the same day as he had his head cu in the posstub to get washed. It was for workmen to have their clothes w time, as they became heavy and gre NOBLE CROSS-EXAMI Cross-examined by Mr Scott-Fox: 31st October he was not out of th

---

Point to Ponder

Once again, 'reasonable force' was at issue in a case involving violence, when Joseph William Noble's counsel argued that even if Noble was the man who entered Windy Nook Co-op, and even if he was armed with a revolver, he would have had just cause to defend himself by the best means he could if he felt his life was threatened – as he would, when tackled by three men and struck on the head several times by a butcher's steel. He would argue the gun was in his pocket and had not been used to threaten anyone, and only after serious assault on his person had he drawn it and fired at his assailants. There can be no doubt that he was struck with unnecessary force. But then, it's easy to cast judgement when outside of the situation.

Assuming Noble was the killer – and the evidence of identification was flawed – he may indeed have drawn the gun in self defence. But he took it upon himself to be armed in the first place, so it could be reasonably argued he brought about his own fate. The jury would have had no sympathy, which is not to say their judgement was correct. Assessment of facts, not emotion, should be the means of interpreting the law.

An Unhappy New Year

Joseph William Noble did not die alone on the scaffold. Another man, Robert Lawman, died with him, condemned to death for the murder of his lover, Amelia Bell Wood. The case was described as 'a sordid story of drink, domestic unhappiness and shame, with tragedy as their sequel'. Lawman was a Cumberland man. He was 32, married, and had left his wife and sons four years previously, since when he had lived with Amelia. She worked as a barmaid. Lawman worked too, cleaning tramcars as well as down the pit, and had good cause to complain about her conduct if, as he explained at his trial, 'she was out all hours, and coming home after two o'clock in the morning drunk'.

On 30th December, 1907, Amelia turned up at the Gateshead home of Mrs Sinclair in Hyde Park Street, seeking lodgings. Mrs Sinclair took her in. The following day – New Year's Eve – Amelia went out and just before midnight returned to her lodgings with a man she introduced to Mrs Sinclair as her husband. The pair remained in the parlour all night and through to about noon on New Year's Day, when Amelia ordered breakfast for two. As in so many 'domestic' situations, after love comes war, and when Amelia screamed, and Mrs Sinclair could not get a reply to her knock, she went for the police. When they arrived they forced their way into the room where they found a scene of carnage.

---THE NEWCASTLE DAILY JOURNAL, WEDNESDAY, MARCH 25, 1908.

EXECUTIONS AT DURHAM.

:o:

Windy Nook and Gateshead Murders Expiated.

THE LAST PENALTY.

A double hanging took place within the precincts of Durham Gaol, yesterday, when Joseph William Noble, a blacksmith, and Robert Lawman, a miner, paid the extreme penalty of the law for the murders committed respectively at Windy Nook and Gateshead.

The history and details of the respective crimes have already recently been recapitulated in these columns.

Noble and Lawman retired to rest on Monday night at the usual hour, and rose early yesterday morning. Dressing themselves in the clothes which they wore at the trial, these having taken the place during the night of the prison garb, both men, at seven o'clock, were visited by the prison chaplain, and afterwards attended a short service in the prison chapel. Afterwards they each partook of a light breakfast, consist-

THE LATE DOWAGER TWEEDMOUTH.

Funeral in Londo⸱

Amid unmistakable tokens of affecti⸱ the remains of the late Dowager Lady mother of the First Lord of the Admira⸱ yesterday at Kensal Green, in the va⸱ members of the family lie buried.

Her ladyship died on Friday last at dence of her son in Whitehall, and it that the funeral cortege set out yeste⸱ Green Cemetery.

The coffin was borne upon an open ⸱ entirely hidden from sight by a mas⸱ cream satin edged with gold lace, and w⸱ it worked in gold, which extended ⸱ whole length. The roof of the funera⸱ with beautiful flowers which had been and friends.

A number of carriages followed the ⸱ mouth (son), the Countess of Aberdee⸱ Viceroy of Ireland (son-in-law), Lord son), Lady Haddo, Lady Marjorie daughter), Lord Ridley and the Hor⸱

Double Execution – Robert Lawman and Joseph William Noble were hanged together at Durham.

79

On the floor lay the body of Amelia Bell Wood. There was a wound on her forehead and her throat had been cut. Nearby lay Robert Lawman, who also had a throat wound, but not life-threatening. A bloodstained knife was found on the window sill, and a broken bottle lay by the bed. The officers attended to Lawman's injury and he was taken to hospital. He said, 'I loved her. I killed her. I will swing for her.' He was right. At the Durham Assizes the chief constable detailed the facts of the case, then Lawman had his say.

He said that after Amelia had left their house he had shaved, dressed in smart clothes and met her. She was so drunk, he said, she didn't recognise him. He had taken a knife with him, so that if she would not speak to him he would commit suicide. She had seen the knife, picked it up and said, 'I will fettle you', and he had grasped it, sustaining cuts to his fingers, whereupon she slashed his throat and cut his jaw. He had hit her on the face with a broken bottle to defend himself. He had not used the knife to injure Amelia at all. After a 'guilty' verdict, the judge passed the only sentence possible. Lawman replied, 'I thank you, my Lord'. On 24th March, 1908, Robert Lawman met Joe Noble at the scaffold.

MURDER OF A YOUNG INNOCENT

The Wardley Hotel, Bill Quay. A drinking haunt of Thomas Nicholson, and venue of the inquest into the murder of Mary Ina Stewart.

'You can't let the kids out of your sight these days.'

How often have we heard that, when news of yet another murder of a child comes courtesy of your television or newspaper? Young victims, strangled, beaten or otherwise killed, usually during acts of sexual perversion, or to ensure their silence after they have suffered. We remember how, as youngsters we played in the parks, wandered the fields, roamed free unsupervised without the need for supervision of worried parents. Kids were safe in the old days – weren't they...?

It wasn't safe for seven-year old Mary Ina Stewart, of Bill Quay, near Pelaw, as events would prove on a summer's evening in 1902. Mary was one of six children to James Stewart, a widower who, alone, was bringing up his children. It wasn't easy for a brickmaker who worked long hours. The family lived at 16 Joel Terrace, and Frederick Stewart, James's brother, lived only a few hundred yards away in Gosforth Terrace, on the other side of higher ground known locally as Hilly Fields.

James Stewart last saw Mary alive at 10.30 a.m. on Saturday, 16th August, after which he went to Hexham, 20 miles away, where he

SHOCKING TRAGEDY AT BILL QUAY.

A LITTLE GIRL MURDERED.

A shocking discovery was made at Bill Quay, near Pelaw, yesterday afternoon, when the dead body of a girl was found in a brickyard at that place, circumstances pointing to the fact that the child had been murdered. The name of the child was Mary Stewart. She was seven yeads of age, and her parents reside at No. 8, Joel Terrace, Bill Quay. She had been missing since Sunday.

It is stated that the girl was sent a message on Saturday and never returned. There was great anxiety on the part of her relatives, who failed to discover any trace of her until yesterday afternoon, when her dead body, as stated, was found in a brickyard near Messrs Wood and Skinner's shipbuilding yard, between Felling and Hebburn. There were several severe cuts about the body, which was seen by Dr Mackay of Pelaw.

The affair is being investigated by Superintendent

spent the day working. When he got home at 10.30 p.m. he discovered Mary was not there, but was not unduly concerned as he expected her to be at her uncle's. So he waited, probably cross at Mary's lateness, until finally he went to his brother's house only to be told she had left to walk home at 7.30.

Now there was cause for alarm, and James Stewart wasted no time in getting a search party together, neighbours who searched the streets and the nearby Cat Dene quarry. They searched all night, and through Sunday, but there was no sign of Mary. They were still searching on Monday when the news came through, and James's worst fears were realised. Mary's body had been found in Wood & Skinner's disused brickyard. Her body, still fully clothed, was carefully concealed by grass and was 'shockingly disfigured and mutilated, with injuries inflicted by a madman'. James Stewart picked his daughter up and carried her home.

Two factors, I would venture, differ from the situation then and that of similar circumstances today. One, a century ago fewer people travelled far; no-one at Bill Quay would have owned a car. And two, forensic science techniques in those days did not include the ability to compare blood groups, or carry out DNA profiling. In short, the offender would almost certainly be local, but neither his blood or semen could be compared scientifically.

They opened the inquest at the Wardley Hotel on the Monday, when the coroner, A.T. Shepherd, strangely remarked that he 'sincerely hoped such a thing would not occur again for a long time', implying he expected it would someday. Then, on the Tuesday morning, the police made an early arrest. The suspect was Thomas Nicholson, 23, a cartman employed at nearby Woodgate Farm. A Bill Quay man, he lived with his mother in nearby Back Ann Street. When he appeared before the Gateshead magistrates the court was told the prisoner, when arrested, had said he'd spent the Saturday night drinking at a public house where he had remained until closing time. A knife had been found in his pocket and sent to the county analyst, and bloodstains had been discovered on the front of his shirt. He had nothing to say when charged with the murder of Mary.

A post mortem examination was conducted by Dr Prentice. Mary had been 'outraged', the court was told, an Edwardian way of saying she had been raped without actually saying the word. Cause of death was suffocation and loss of blood. The county analyst, William Stock, said he had examined some of Nicholson's clothing and found it to be bloodstained, and that there was dried blood on the knife taken from the prisoner. Nicholson was committed for trial and the case opened at Durham Assizes in November before Mr Justice Channell. Nicholson's movements on the day of the murder were vital to the outcome of the case; he needed an alibi, showing he was elsewhere when Mary was taken. The prosecution, of course, had to prove 'beyond reasonable doubt' that he abducted and killed her, even if Nicholson couldn't prove anything.

THE BILL QUAY MURDER,

OPENING OF THE INQUEST.

A YOUNG MAN ARRESTED.

An inquest was opened, last evening, at the Wardley Hotel, Bill Quay, on the body of Mary Ina Stewart, who was found in a disused quarry on Monday afternoon under circumstances already reported.

Mr A. T. Shephard (coroner), said he proposed only to take evidence of identification and adjourn the inquest for a time sufficient for the police to make further inquiries.

James Stewart, brickmaker, residing at 16, Joel Terrace, Bill Quay, identified the body as that of his daughter. She was seven years of age in June last. He last saw her alive about 10.30 on Saturday morning. She was then at home. At 12.55 witness left Pelaw for Hexham. He returned home about 10.30 at night. He heard the child was at his brother's house, Gosforth Terrace, Pelaw. Witness waited a while, thinking his brother would bring the child over, and then went to the house, but found she was not there. He was informed that she had left at 7.30 p.m., and that his brother had accompanied her along part of the road. Witness returned home, got a search party up, and went through the Cat Dene Quarry and around about the village. They searched all night but found no trace of her. The search was continued on Sunday and

Dr Mackay of Pelaw told the court he had examined Mary on three occasions: at the murder scene on the Monday, when he estimated that Mary had been dead for two days, suggesting she had been dead since Saturday, the day of her disappearance, her house afterwards and when he assisted in the post mortem examination. He said that Mary had been struck on the head with a blunt instrument, causing unconsciousness. There were marks around her mouth and nostrils, consistent with someone trying to stifle any screams, and she had suffocated as a result of this and loss of blood caused by the wounds to her skull and 'certain other parts of her body'; a knife had been used to cut her genitals to allow penetration. An horrific crime perpetrated on an innocent child – but was Thomas Nicholson the killer?

Mary had a friend, 11-year old Johanna Scott. On the day Mary disappeared the two left Mary's house at Joel Street together at 6.50 p.m. and walked by way of Hilly Fields to Mary's uncle's house at

84

Gosforth Terrace. There they remained until 7.30 when they left together to walk home, Johanna to Heworth, Mary to Joel Street. It must have been Mary that a passer-by, Alice Nichols, saw, as she too walked over Hilly Fields. Describing her as 'a young girl with golden hair', she said she was walking in the same direction (towards Bill Quay), some way behind, and a 'young man' was walking in the opposite direction. She saw the man and the young girl meet and he spoke to her. Then he took her hand and they walked off towards the quarry. She was not able to identify the 'young man', but felt sure the body of Mary Stewart (which she was shown) was the girl she had seen. But, again, was the man Thomas Nicholson?

On the day of Mary's disappearance Nicholson was with James Dinning, a miner, who lived at 4 Swinburne Terrace, Bill Quay. Their houses backed on to one another's and the two men were friends and drinking partners. That afternoon they were together at the Wardley Hotel, and on leaving around 4.30 p.m. they agreed to meet up later at the Masons Arms, Felling Shore, which they did at about five o'clock, staying until 6.30 when they went to the home of a man named Holmes, before returning going to Dinning's house. Thereafter, around 7.30 p.m. – around the time Mary and Johanna were leaving Mary's uncle's house in Gosforth Terrace – Nicholson went to his mother's house, alone, followed just two minutes later by Dinning who 'saw him in the kitchen'.

About this time another miner, Robert Felton, saw Nicholson walking down Back Ann Street towards his house. He saw him again five minutes later, as he left the house and walked in the direction of Hilly Fields. Dinning checked drinking haunts, finding no trace of Nicholson, which he thought strange as he expected Nicholson would rejoin him to continue their drinking session. He went home and waited for his friend who did not appear.

After Dinning had gone off to search, his wife, Christina, looked out of her kitchen window to see Thomas Nicholson emerge from his house with a piece of bread in his hand. She watched him nibbling the bread as he headed off in the direction of Hilly Fields. He was wearing a dark suit. Later, at 9.15, she was chatting to a friend at her back door when she saw him again. He was no longer wearing his coat or vest. He passed them by without speaking, went into his house, reappeared after a few minutes and asked her if her husband was in. He wasn't (he was still looking for him in the local pubs). Nicholson was also seen by Martin Mackay, another carter, who asked him where he was going. To Felling, to buy a new suit, Nicholson told him. Mackay thought Nicholson was drunk and advised him to go home. Nicholson's response was to punch the wall.

No person was able to put Nicholson at the scene of the murder, except perhaps Alice Nichols, who had seen a man and a golden-haired little girl on Hilly Fields, although she could not positively identify the man. But Thomas Douglas, who lived in Gosforth Terrace and who knew Nicholson, was crossing Hilly Fields on an errand for his mother

The Cricketers, Bill Quay. Another of Nicholson's watering holes ...

when he saw Nicholson 'walking backwards and forwards' near the quarry.

The police established that the suit Nicholson had worn on Saturday evening had been pawned for six shillings, a not uncommon occurrence. The pawnbroker was Joseph Lightfoot. Nicholson had collected his suit on the Monday, and when the police got it they handed it to the county analyst who found blood on both coat and trousers.

In the end it could not be conclusively proved that Thomas Nicholson had abducted and murdered Mary Stewart; the evidence was circumstantial, no more. Mitchell Innes, for Nicholson, told the court there was 'an unparalleled absence of direct evidence' to connect the prisoner with the crime, and that 'other people were in the neighbourhood that evening too'. Nicholson himself asked the jury not to put too much importance on his bloodstained clothing, saying 'innocent blood is as red as guilty blood'. Such a pity they had not the technology to group the blood, as they would today. The verdict was guilty. Nicholson was hanged at Durham on 16th December, 1902, by two of the Billington brothers, William and John. He never confessed to the crime.

Point to Ponder

The murder of a child stirs up feelings of anger and revenge perhaps more than any other crime. The most monstrous things unimaginable happen to innocents, deeds so wicked, so incomprehensible. The little girl or boy, lured away by the stranger and subjected to perverted and depraved acts, and murdered either in the course of these or to ensure later identification of their killer cannot be made; or a child killed within the family home, sexually abused and murdered by a stepfather perhaps, or simply neglected and left to die by an indifferent mother, too often failed by so-called caring agencies.

Are these offenders in their right mind? Those like Thomas Nicholson, in every other way a law abiding, decent citizen, are they driven by some form of perverted madness, incomprehensible to the rest of us? Others, these days, are just as depraved, and thanks to technology have much to gain from their despicable acts: paedophiles who video record rape and violation and murder so that they may sell their wares to an eager market, customers inside or outside prison walls eager to pay for this new form of sexual gratification.

Such people should never be freed, surely. And if they are, and if again they torture and take innocent life, let those who freed them take the consequences. Accountability should focus their minds admirably.

'Never Take Sweets From A Stranger'

This sound advice to a child could have been taken from the circumstances surrounding the murder of seven-year old Caroline Winter, who was led to her death by an unknown man near her home at Seaham in 1889. Caroline lived with her disabled father, a former miner. On the night of 2nd August she was playing in Back

Back North Terrace, Seaham.

Featherbed Rocks, Seaham. Featherbed Rock, which stood offshore, has disappeared. It was climbed by locals and visitors – including Lord Byron.

North Terrace with her friend, Ann Cowell, when the man, wearing a shabby coat, approached and spoke to Caroline with the promise of money to buy sweets. Sixpence was mentioned, a lot of money to an impressionable little girl. He led her off, followed at first by Ann who in the darkness became scared and ran home alone.

Next morning Caroline's battered body, her arms bruised from blows sustained in her pathetic attempts to protect herself from repeated blows to her head, was found near Featherbed Rock, a large, prominent landmark attached to the mainland where today's crumbling cliffs are now protected from the sea by huge granite boulders. She was reported to have been 'outraged' – that word again – then moved from the place of her murder to make it appear

Lord Byron, 'the darling of London society', was married at Seaham.

she had drowned. Caroline was described as 'an innocent child, who was killed and mutilated to satisfy one man's fiendish lust'. The crime was never solved. One moment she was playing in the street, the next she was gone. Is anything more wicked?

In 1815, Lord Byron, 'the darling of London society', came to Seaham, where he married an heiress, Anne Isabella Milbanke. During his stay in the town, Byron enjoyed scrambling up Featherbed Rock with his bride. For this, the rock may have enjoyed a lasting, romantic image. Sadly, such a notion died with the tragic events at the end of the century. Now the rock has gone, taken by the sea as though to cast into forgettable history it's bitter-sweet memories.

This modern-day monolith may serve as a monument to murdered Caroline Winter.

'IT'S A DOMESTIC!'

The Cross Keys public house, Washington.

'It's a domestic'. So often the reaction of the police to violence perpetrated usually by a husband on his wife, a male on a female partner. A wrong reaction, it must be said. Where is the justice in accepting that if a woman is punched in a nightclub it's a crime, in the kitchen that's OK? Today, police forces' attitude to 'domestics' has changed, or should have. Officers deal with an incident promptly, without pacifying a drunken aggressor; and many forces have 'domestic violence officers' who work with other agencies, offering support to both parties, including confidential advice to the 'battered wife' who needs help but has been too scared to ask, and a structured approach in the prosecution of her aggressor. Let it be said that most 'domestic violence' is not perpetrated by husbands who turn up from the pub drunk and start beating wives and smashing windows; it is a sober, calculated, brutal crime, carried out behind closed doors. Those women who suffered in silence, the majority, in their homes at the hands – and fists – of bullying husbands had no-one to turn to; the police would require a statement before making an arrest (if they did), leaving the victim to go home to her husband, now on bail for beating her up! Such cases can never be accurately recorded. Like an iceberg, where only the very tip appears above the water, the majority of domestic violence crimes are hidden from view.

Police, reluctant to get involved, endeavoured instead to keep the peace before leaving a domestic incident to deal with more 'important' things. After all, the warring parties would make up in the morning, or next week; she would withdraw her complaint and her willingness to testify, and all the work done in arresting, charging and processing the offender would have been a waste of time. Why doesn't she leave him anyway? they might ask, based on the supposed fact that a man is the aggressor, the woman the victim of his aggression. So it is, usually. But not always.

George Richard Drysdale, a coal miner, lived with his wife, Eleanor Ann Drysdale, at Washington. He was 29, she 34. They had one child. Eleanor's violent conduct towards her husband was commonplace; she was known to threaten him with kitchen knives, and Drysdale had a scar on his head to prove it. Neighbours had seen him hiding knives, especially when Eleanor was drunk, which was also commonplace. George Drysdale was a peaceful man who had learned to live with his wife's intemperate habits; as long as he could thwart her violent endeavours with knives all would be well. Or so he must have thought.

Saturday, 5th April, 1902, was George's day off, and at eleven o'clock that morning he was outside, staining a piece of wood he would use to mend a chair, when Eleanor asked him for the money to pay the rent. He gave her eight shillings, and said to next door neighbour, Terence Joyce, 'Do you think she will pay all the rent?' She returned after ten minutes with the news that the rent was paid but she had kept a shilling for a drink. Drysdale and Joyce were neighbours and friends who got along fine. They'd known each other about ten years. Joyce witnessed events between the Drysdales that morning, as well as George's oft-time endeavours to hide kitchen knives.

Later, that day, Joyce went to Washington, and returned home at 5 o'clock, whereupon he fell asleep in a chair. The next time he would see George Drysdale was when he was awakened at 9.15 that evening by the man himself who addressed him with the words, 'Well, Teddy, I think I have fettled her this time.' 'Who?' asked the still sleepy Joyce. 'Nellie,' said George. 'Go and look at her.' Indeed he had fettled her; George Drysdale had just battered his wife to death with a poker. 'Shall I go for the doctor or the police?' asked Joyce. 'Please yourself,' said George.

George Drysdale never denied killing his wife. But at his trial for murder at Durham Assizes the following July he pleaded not guilty to her murder. His account of events that Saturday afternoon and evening was told in full to judge and jury, along with testimony from others – Terence Joyce, George's sister-in-law, Dorothy Jane Drysdale (Eleanor and Dorothy married brothers, so their were no name-changes), Thomas Black and Florence King. Dorothy described her sister as 'intemperate and immoral'; she said she was a violent woman who often threatened her husband and herself. She knew of George

ALLEGED WIFE MURDER AT WASHINGTON.

George Richard Drysdale, a miner, residing at Washington went into the house of a neighbour named Joyce on Saturday evening and said, "I believe I have done it this time." The man spoken to proceeded to the dwelling next door, only to find that the remark was literally true. Mrs Drysdale was lying on the floor, her head terribly injured, and she was half covered with blood. Dr Jacques was called in, but the woman was past help, and she died in about half an hour. The police immediately arrested the husband, and took possession of a piece of iron which lay on the floor. This had been used in the house as a poker, and as it was bespattered with blood, it was evident that it was the weapon with which the crime had been committed. The accused man is stated to be 30 years of age, and his wife nearly four years older. Their one child is three years of age. The unfortunate couple had resided in Washington for some years, but their

Drysdale's scar, and how he came to have it. Thomas Black, another miner, said he was in the snug of the Cross Keys public house that evening when George and his wife came in and sat nearby. He said George was 'OK' – meaning he was sober – but that Eleanor was already drunk.

Florence King was also seated in the snug. She confirmed the Drysdales' presence and that Eleanor was 'the worse for drink'. At one point a child had been asleep on Eleanor's knee, and around 8.30 she got up and told her husband she was going home. 'Why?' asked George. 'Because I am drunk,' replied Eleanor, whereupon she fell back to her seat and the child fell to the floor. George picked the child up, and Florence King opened the door for them. The Drysdales left, and Eleanor promptly fell down outside. That was about 9 o'clock. Fifteen minutes later she was dying.

She was found by Dr Jacques (called by Terence Joyce) and Sergeant John Lambert, lying on the kitchen floor with her head on the fender. She was alive, but in a 'dying condition'. Dr Jacques told the court it was 'a terrible and horrible sight', and that Drysdale had said 'I did it. I am not going to deny it'. Drysdale showed him a poker, the murder weapon. It was 37 inches long and weighed over 5 lb. Eleanor Drysdale died at 11 p.m.

Defending Drysdale against the charge of murder, Mr Shortt, barrister, said the crime should be reduced to manslaughter. He invited the jury to look at the Drysdales' 'previous history', as well as their conduct on the fateful day. He suggested they should consider George Drysdale had acted in self defence; he had been threatened with a knife and had caused injury to his wife to save himself. Two witnesses would say a knife had been found at the scene and one, George Drysdale's nephew, Robert, 16, had given Terence Joyce a white handled knife which he had found on the floor, at the Drysdales' house. It was considered to be the weapon used by Eleanor to threaten George.

Exactly what took place in the Drysdale household could only be known to two people, George and Eleanor. George Drysdale told the court that when he and his wife returned from the Cross Keys he had twice asked her to 'fettle his supper'. In those days for her to do so was expected. Her response was to threaten to put a knife through him, quite believable in the light of past events. She picked up a knife and walked towards him to stab him. He knocked it from her hand, flung her to the floor. She came again with the knife, so he took up the poker and 'felled her'. After that, he said, he could not remember anything.

The jury returned a verdict of not guilty to murder, guilty to manslaughter. George Drysdale was sentenced to 15 years penal servitude.

Point to Ponder

Was George Drysdale guilty of manslaughter and not murder, as charged? His defence was self defence, protecting himself against his drunken wife who was armed with a knife, and who had injured him or threatened to injure him in the past.

If he was acting reasonably in his own defence, the verdict should have been one of acquittal. Either he did act reasonably or he did not. But was his conduct 'reasonable'? By his own admission, he first thwarted his wife's attempt to stab him by pushing her drunken form to the floor. She came again so he struck her on the head with a heavy poker. Comes the question: when he pushed her down, could he not have left the room, made his escape (as doubtless he had done many times before)? Was striking his hapless wife with a poker his only alternative, a fatal blow struck with 'I've had enough' written all over it? On the evidence given George Drysdale was guilty of murder, whatever his wife's violent history.

Ruth Ellis was the last woman to hang in Britain, on 13th July, 1955. She allegedly suffered continuous abuse by her boyfriend and gunned him down on a London street – the ultimate response to being subjected to 'domestic violence'?

'She Was A Dead Wrong Woman'

Testifying at the inquest into the murder at Sunderland of 51-year old widow, Mary Ann Dixon, her common law husband and killer, William Hall, 66, wanted the public to know the truth: that she had left him five times, taking with her food, including tea and sugar, as well as a comb and bobbins, and she had pawned the 'wedding ring' and clothing he had bought her and for which he had given her money to redeem.

Hall worked as a brass finisher in a Sunderland shipyard. He and Mrs Dixon had cohabited together 'on and off', for about two years. But she kept leaving him, and even the prosecution at Hall's trial conceded it was she who was the cause of their constant quarrelling. In September, 1919, she left him again, choosing instead to live and work as night-woman at a lodging house. On Wednesday, 5th November, annoyed and depressed, Hall called on Mary Ann's sister, Elizabeth Adamson, saying he was going to meet her at six o'clock, saying 'don't say anything' as he drew his finger across his throat in a gesture of apparent intent.

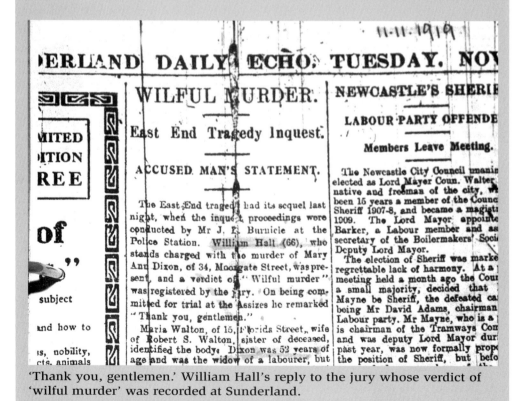

'Thank you, gentlemen.' William Hall's reply to the jury whose verdict of 'wilful murder' was recorded at Sunderland.

At six, Hall and Mary Ann went for a drink in the Tynemouth Castle pub, and were evidently on friendly terms. Around 10 p.m. Mrs Adamson, concerned about Hall's 'bad temper', went to his lodgings on the ground floor of 34 Moorgate Street, where she heard the reassuring sound of Hall and Mary Ann chatting. When she returned at one o'clock the following day, she found the door and shutter fastened, as they were still at 10.30 that evening. She called the police.

Mary Ann Dixon was found inside on the bed with her throat cut. Hall was in the house, and said simply, 'I know I am guilty. I wish I had killed myself when I was at it'. He explained that Mary Ann had wanted to return to the lodging house, but he could not let her go. At trial, he put forward a defence of provocation, saying he had been 'seized by sudden impulse and acted in a frenzy' by Mary Ann's desire to leave. The judge disagreed, saying there was no provocation in this case to justify a charge of manslaughter. Quite so: Mary Ann had every right to do as she pleased. Hall, found guilty of murder, said, 'If there is nothing gained in what I did, I can stand under God and say there was nothing lost, for she was a

Sunderland, about 1916.

dead wrong woman'. Dead indeed, as he would be. When sentenced to death, Hall replied, 'Thank you, my Lord'. He was hanged at Durham on 23rd March, 1920, as the cathedral clock chimed eight o'clock. It is recorded that the lever was pulled on the third stroke of the hour.

Sentenced to Death. 'Guilty under provocation' said the accused.

AN ACUTE CASE OF
PHOSPHORUS POISONING

Mary Elizabeth Wilson.

'Mrs Mary Elizabeth Wilson has been arrested on a charge of murdering her husband, Ernest Lawrence George Wilson. She will appear before a special magistrates' court in the morning.' These were the solemn words of Inspector Albert Mitchell of the Durham Constabulary following the arrest of the recently-widowed 'Mrs Wilson', as she would become infamously known, on Wednesday, 11th December, 1957.

Mrs Wilson, 66, had been widowed twice in just five weeks, three times in all, counting the death of her first husband less than two years before, as well as 'losing' her live-in lodger four months after that. How it was that so many died without raising suspicion seems strange, but it may be said that in the end Mary Wilson's greed led to her undoing and ultimate conviction for the last two murders, and the sentence of death passed at Leeds Assizes in March, 1958.

She was born Mary Elizabeth Cassidy, in 1892. Tragedy struck early for her when her fiancé, John, a coal miner, was killed in the West Stanley pit disaster of 1909. Mary left school at 14, and went into service and later, at 22, now working for a wealthy builder she fell for his son, John Knowles, a chimney sweep, and the pair decided to marry. Marry they did, but then he was called up along with thousands of other young men to fight in the Great War. Unlike so many of those thousands he came home, and they settled down to a life together in Hebburn.

Alas, not happily. Whether they weren't made for each other isn't known but, over the years, they ended up sleeping in separate rooms although Mary Knowles, as she then was, still cooked for her husband and carried out her wifely duties. Then Mary took in a lodger, John George Russell, at 65 younger than her husband by ten years. 'I might as well cook for three as well as two,' said Mary, and she did. But her culinary skills were not the sole interest of Mr Russell who came to share his landlady's bed, an arrangement that evidently suited Mr Knowles, or at least was one he tolerated.

Things ticked along for a time until Mary's husband complained of feeling unwell with stomach pains and vomiting. This was unusual, as he had always enjoyed good health. Mary called the doctor who prescribed medicine in liquid form. She told a friend that 'the medicine didn't seem to be doing much good' and she was right. On 31st August, 1956, John Knowles died, aged 76.

The funeral took place without fuss, which was hardly surprising at the passing of a man his age. Mary, now the mourning widow and perhaps feeling restless, sold the house and moved into another not far away at 18 Collingwood Street, along with her lodger-cum-lover, John Russell. They lived together for five months when, just before Christmas he too began to complain of sickness. The doctor was called, and medicine was prescribed and administered by Mary, as well as hot soup, ideal on cold winter's evenings. Alas, in January, John Russell passed on. He left £46 to Mary.

Both men had died from 'natural causes', at least that's what the death certificates said. Apart from perhaps wondering for a short time about the remarkable passing of two men within five months of each other, there was no cause to suspect anything amiss. Things soon got back to normal and Mary soon got started on the quest for another man to share her life, this time somebody with money. For, as later events would prove, the woman was a ruthless killer and there was little point in doing away with the men in her life for a pittance.

It wasn't long before Mary had identified her next husband. Oliver James Leonard, a retired estate agent, lived in lodgings with Mr and Mrs Connolly at Hebburn. At 76 Mr Leonard was probably attracted to the younger woman. At any rate it wasn't long before he moved in with Mary. She must have considered a retired estate agent quite a catch, but Mr Leonard would not agree to 'sign over' any of his money to Mary, a situation naturally not to her liking and she ended up at the Connolly's door demanding they 'get the old bugger out of my house'. Mrs Connolly said she would be delighted to have Mr Leonard back, but the next day Mary called again to say they had made up and there was no need.

Witnesses in the Wilson case Mrs Connolly (left) and Mrs Russell.

In fact, things went well for Mary, for didn't she and Oliver marry that very year, on 20th September, 1956, at Jarrow Registry Office. Things went less well for Oliver; thirteen days later he was dead. But not before, in between the marriage and his death, Mrs Leonard – that's Mary – had called to see one James Henry Haws, an insurance agent, of Jarrow. She told Mr Haws that she wanted to insure her husband. Alas for Mary, Mr Haws told her he was too old to insure.

In the early hours of 3rd October, Mary called on her neighbours, the Shrivingtons, saying her husband, Oliver, had fallen out of bed. Mr Shrivington and his sister went to the house and put Mr Leonard back. Mr Leonard was unable to speak and was very white. Mary Shrivington tried to hand a cup of tea to him, but he knocked the cup away. At 11 a.m. Mary sent a message to a Mrs Russell, of Edgar Street, Jarrow (no relation to Mary's now-dead lover), saying her husband was ill and could she call? When Mrs Russell arrived Mary invited her too into the room where her husband was. Mrs Russell saw him in bed. As she would later testify, 'I noticed that Mr Leonard was twisting his face, taking a deep breath and then stopping. He did this four or five times. I was in the room when he died. I laid him out. Dr Leydon came a short while after then I went home'.

Dr John Leydon, G.P., confirmed that he had seen Mr Leonard on 1st October, when he complained of 'chest trouble and senile debility'. 'There was nothing in my examination which made me suspect that any question of poisoning,' he said. At no time did the doctor visit the house, before or after Mr Leonard's death, yet he issued a death certificate listing the cause of death as 'myocardial degeneration and nephritis (kidney disease)' based on his examination of his patient two days before. Mary received about £50 as payment for old and sundry insurance policies.

George Leonard, her late husband's son, called on Mary. He asked her to confirm that she had married his father and enquired of the circumstances of his death. Then, as he would later admit, he 'lost his temper a bit', admitting he 'more or less accused her' of inveigling his father into a marriage of convenience, adding that he could not have been in his right mind marrying her. Then he asked if he could see his father's will, which Mary said was with her solicitor, adding that his father had left everything to her. In court, George Leonard admitted that the reason he called to see Mary was to enquire about the will. It seems Oliver Leonard's estate was the sole and mutually shared concern of his wife and son.

It may seem strange that the death of three men in Mary's life had not attracted suspicion, but the first two were considered bad luck, and the third happened in another location, just far enough away to go unnoticed. As for Mary, her wicked ways had earned her less than a hundred pounds and a few pieces of furniture. Given that even she must have realised she could not keep on killing people forever, she would have resolved to make the next one worthwhile. She waited a whole year before choosing victim number four.

Chief Inspector Alexander Mitchell.

Mr R.G. Barrow, insurance agent.

Dr William Stewart, pathologist.

Ernest George Wilson, 75, was a retired engineer. He had £100 invested in the Co-op, he was insured for £50 and he had a 'nice home' (which turned out to be a council house at 26 Rectory Road, Windy Nook). On 28th October, 1957, Mary and Ernest Wilson were married at Jarrow Registry Office; Mary sold her house and moved into her new husband's home. On 11th November, Mr Wilson's G.P., Dr Wallace, was called and Mr Wilson was confined to bed. The doctor suspected a heart ailment and prescribed pills and cough mixture. The following day the doctor was recalled to the house where he found Mr Wilson dead.

Dr Wallace concluded that death was due to muscular degeneration of the heart and made out a death certificate. Mary's fourth husband had lived for just 15 days after they were married (two more than her third). Belatedly, you might think, the rumours started. Local sympathy at Mrs Wilson losing two husbands in just over a fortnight evaporated when someone realised other men in her life had died in quick succession; and the death of Ernest Wilson had been highlighted in a sympathetic newspaper article, for he had been a sad, lonely figure after the death of his first wife, Clara, and now, having remarried and at last found happiness he had passed away so quickly. They chatted in the pubs and in the corner shop – wasn't it suspicious?

The police must have thought so for on 30th November they were granted permission to exhume the bodies of Oliver James Leonard and Ernest George Wilson. The game was up for Mary who stayed awhile in the Albert Hotel, Hebburn. In the light of events she could hardly have stayed at home while the police sought evidence in the form of the pathologist's reports on the two deceased men (one wonders when things had got that far why she wasn't staying in the cells at the police station). It wasn't long in coming. The pathologist, Dr William Stewart, who carried out the post mortem on Mr Leonard, was satisfied that 'death was not due to the cause named on the medical certificate'. He took samples of stomach, intestine and liver and sent them to the Home Office Forensic Science Laboratory at Gosforth where Dr Barclay discovered 'elemental phosphates and bran', two substitutes only found together in rat poison. Cause of death: phosphate poisoning. The same results were discovered in the body of Mr Wilson.

It would be remarkable that both husbands would have self-administered rat poison after a period of about a year. How it might have been given it isn't known, for Mary never said, but she probably slipped it into their medicine; it would have made tea very bitter, although knocking the cup from Mrs Shrivington's hand tends to show some, at least, was taken by Mr Leonard that way. Maybe they got so ill they couldn't tell. Mary Wilson was charged with the murders of both men.

Rose Heilbron, Q.C., defended Mary Wilson at her trial at Leeds Assizes. Mary pleaded not guilty to murdering Mr Leonard and Mr Wilson. She was not charged with murdering her first husband or Mr Russell, who had been dead longer and in whose bodies it was more difficult to detect the presence of poison. The prosecution would have reasoned a conviction (or two) for later murders would see her hang just as readily. Dr Stewart said Mr Wilson's death was due to poisoning. He told the court 'the congestion in the gullet and the intestines and the yellowish discolouration of the liver tissues' drove him to that conclusion. Liver was normally chocolate-coloured and liver tissues are susceptible to poison and changes take place rapidly, resulting in degeneration accompanied by a yellowish appearance. There were other symptoms. 'Phosphorus in its elemental form is not found in the human body,' said Dr Stewart, adding he knew of no way it could get into the body except through the mouth. This was an acute case of phosphorus poisoning, and death would have occurred within two days.

Mary Cook gave evidence. She said that from May, 1955 to May, 1956, she was employed at the Jarrow and Hebburn Co-operative Society's chemist's shop. Rodine rat poison was sold there. She was asked if she knew Mrs Wilson. She did. Where had she seen her before? As a customer in the shop. Grace Liddle, a friend of Mrs Wilson, told the court that on the day before Ernest Wilson's death she had seen his gold watch in Mrs Wilson's shopping bag. 'She was trying to sell it,' she said, adding that she had visited the house the following day where she had seen Mr Wilson's body. She had not known he was dead and had to be revived with smelling salts. Asked to describe the Wilson household, Mrs Liddle said, 'A dog kennel is cleaner.'

Mary Wilson declined to give evidence on her own behalf. This meant she could not be questioned. Such conduct must always weaken a defendant's case; if innocent, why not testify? Mention was made, by the defence, of a bottle of tablets marked 'poison', found by police in

Rose Heilbron QC, who defended   Mr Justice Hinchcliffe, trial judge.
Mrs Wilson at her trial.

the Wilson household. The prosecution had not mentioned these, indeed they had not even been brought to court and the judge ordered their production. A case of not wanting to introduce anything likely to cause doubt in the mind of the jury, perhaps. That's all the defence needs to do: cause doubt. They don't have to prove anything. That's the job of the prosecution. The 56 tablets were to help prevent nose-bleeding, and were discounted by the jury as the cause of either husband's death

William Dixon, a private detective, told the court he was able to purchase a bottle of 'poison' tablets at a wholesalers. Clearly, the defence was trying to suggest Mr Wilson had taken an overdose of readily-available pills. But there was no accounting for phosphorus in the body and they were clutching at invisible straws. It took the jury an hour and a quarter to return guilty verdicts. The judge sentenced Mary Wilson to death. She was taken to Holloway for sentence to be carried out, only for it to be commuted to life imprisonment by the Home Secretary. She died on 5th December, 1962, aged seventy.

Point to Ponder

Although Mary Wilson was sentenced to death for murdering her second and third husbands, the Home Secretary exercised his power to commute her sentence to life imprisonment. Others hanged for one murder, often born out of a spontaneous, 'domestic' situation, such as a drunken husband killing his wife. Yet Mary Wilson, a cold, calculated killer, who poisoned two (and probably four) men, was spared. Why? Because she was a woman? It is barely conceivable that a man who had murdered two of his wives would have been spared. Because of her age? Perhaps. Sixty-six was 'older' then than now. She wasn't insane, or she would not have been convicted.

'Mrs Wilson.' A kindly face, but did she escape the noose because she was a woman?

Once sentenced, a murderer's fate lay at the whim of a politician in London. He (it was always 'he' then) might be having a good day, an indifferent day, or a wretched day. It cannot be justice when the life of another depends on someone's mood; or, arguably, a victim's family is robbed of seeing someone pay the ultimate penalty. The very least justice should have provided, in the days of capital punishment, was a considered decision by more than one person, the majority decision to stand. What do politicians know of justice anyway!

A Mysterious Motive For Murder

Mary Wilson wasn't the only active serial killer on Tyneside in the 1950s. Peter Thomas Anthony Manuel, 31, was born in New York but moved to the U.K. with his family in 1932, and lived in Glasgow. Manuel was a monster, who for reasons best known to himself arrived by train at Newcastle Central Station at 4.30 a.m. on Saturday, 7th December, 1957. He caught a taxi, driven by 36-year old Sydney Dunn, a single man who lived with his mother and twin brothers in St Thomas's Crescent. Manuel's intentions, and the reason he killed Dunn, will never be known. But the following day Dunn's taxi was found abandoned on the Durham moors near Edmundbyers, and after a brief search his body was found in the heather. His throat had been cut and he had been shot.

Durham police instigated a murder hunt, as back in Glasgow later that month Isabella Cooke, 17, went missing as she set off from her home to go to a dance. Days later, at Uddingston, Peter Smart and Doris, his wife, were found murdered in their bungalow, along with their ten-year old son. All had been shot. Police learned that Peter Manuel was spending new £1 notes, and when they arrested him they discovered the serial numbers were of the same

Serial Killer: Peter Manuel.

He may look like this

Artist's impression of Sydney Dunn's killer.

sequence to the notes paid to Mr Smart when he had cashed recently a cheque.

Manuel confessed to the murder of the Smarts and Isabella Cooke, leading police to the place where he had buried her. He also admitted murdering 17-year old Anne Knielands, whose body had been discovered on a golf course at East Kilbride two years before. Her skull had been smashed in. And Marion Watt, 45, and her sister Margaret, whose bodies were found in their home, along with the body of Vivienne Watt, 16. It seems strange that he should go to Newcastle, where he murdered the only person he met, the driver of the taxi he took at the Central Station. He was convicted of seven murders and hanged at Barlinnie Prison in July, 1958.

Newcastle Central Station today. Taxis still ply for hire.

A DUBIOUS CONVICTION

Sailing ships on the River Wear, Sunderland.

Tuesday, 11th June, 1839. A Prussian sailing ship, *Phoenix*, lies moored on the Wear. Captain and six crew are asleep, save for Daniel Fredrick Muller, 18, second apprentice, whose two-hour watch starts at midnight. All is quiet, as Captain Johan Frederick Berkholdz occupies his cabin on the port side of the vessel. The mate, Jacob Frederich Ehlert, is in his quarters. The cook, John Christian Eichstadt, is due to relieve Muller on watch at 2 a.m.; ship's apprentice, Johann Gustav Wiedman, is due to relieve the cook at 4. One can imagine the scene: the waters of the river gently lapping against the sides of the ship, a dim light or two flickering ashore as the port of Sunderland sleeps.

Then, in the stillness, someone steals into Capt Berkholdz's cabin, takes up an iron hammer, or 'maaker', and strikes the sleeping captain about the head with it, a cold-blooded murder aboard a foreign ship in English waters. Why? and Who? Alas, the answer only to the former is apparent. To the latter there is doubt, but the mate, Jacob Frederich Ehlert, will hang for the crime. As for the captain, his body, attached by a line to a stone weighing 7 stones, ends up in the Wear. The motive was theft of a few bottles of wines and spirits and some money. For the dastardly deed, the mate, Ehlert, would blame the second apprentice, Muller, and Muller would blame Ehlert. It may have been either, or both. But it was Jacob Ehlert, 28, who stood in the dock. Being foreign, he was given the opportunity to have six foreigners on the jury. He declined, probably in the belief that he was about to have a fair trial.

All of the ship's crew spoke only German, so it was necessary to have an interpreter in court, Mr Blech. Since Daniel Muller was apparently believed by the police, insofar as his testimony was accepted as a means of proving the 'guilt' of Ehlert, we will start with his

Ehlert (left) and Muller.

account. Giving 'Queen's Evidence' on 27th July he confirmed he had started watch at midnight when the mate, Ehlert, 'desired me to come down to the captain's cabin'. 'What have I to do there?' asked Muller, to which Ehlert gave no answer but went alone to the cabin from which he returned carrying a bottle of brandy. Both men then had a drink, and it may be that Muller was affected by the alcohol, and it would not be easy for a second apprentice to refuse to do as he was bid. So Muller accompanied Ehlert to the captain's cabin. Inside, Ehlert handed Muller a lantern, which had been covered by a jacket and which, when removed, lit the cabin and showed the captain to be fast asleep in his berth.

Muller said that without warning Ehlert struck the sleeping captain three times on the head with an iron hammer. Muller asked him what he was doing, whereupon Ehlert locked the door. Then, said Muller, Ehlert took a line which he tied around the captain's neck, and dragged his body to the floor. The captain had been wearing two shirts, and Ehlert pulled trousers and stockings on to the body and drew the body into a sack. He opened the cabin door and took the sheet from the captain's bed, at which point Muller said he ran upstairs pursued by Ehlert who threatened to kill him, and told him if he kept quiet he would give him £300, saying he thought the captain would have this amount.

Muller said Ehlert then removed the skylight, hoisted the captain's body through the opening on to the deck and threw it overboard, retaining hold of the line. Ehlert then told Muller to bring the ship's boat around to the stern. Muller did as the mate bid, and they got into the boat. Both men rowed off, dragging the captain's body through the water. Somewhere, said Muller, there was a stone lying on the shore. Ehlert brought it into the boat and tied one end of the line (the other still tied to the captain's body) around the stone. Out in the river, Ehlert, threw the stone into the water, and it dragged the captain's body down. Muller said he noticed the body was divested of trousers and sack, lost as they towed it up the river. It was high water.

Both men returned to the ship at about 2 o'clock – the end of Muller's watch, and the time Eichstadt's watch was due to begin. Ehlert told Muller not to call Eichstadt, that he would do the watch himself. Ehlert ordered Muller to his quarters, then called for him again at 4 o'clock – when Wiedeman was due to start his watch – and told him to 'set the captain ashore'. This was impossible, of course, as the captain had been 'set' elsewhere. But Ehlert told Muller to say he had set the captain ashore when later he was asked, and to say the captain was wearing 'a blue pea coat, a pair of grey trousers, boots and new hat'. If he did not say this he would kill him. Muller said he rowed upriver a short distance, then returned to the ship. Ehlert called Wiedman to the watch and Muller returned to his bunk.

The next day, Ehlert told Muller he had thrown the iron hammer into the river, along with the captain's watch; Muller said he had told the crew he had 'set the captain ashore', as he had been bid. It might have seemed strange that the captain had asked to be set ashore in the middle of the night. Then again, maybe they thought he knew of somewhere in Sunderland worth visiting at such a time.

That morning Ehlert presented Muller with three bottles of spirits – wine, rum and Geneva, and some French and Danish coins, including six 5-franc pieces. Muller put the money in a box and hid it in his berth. He knew the spirits were from the captain's cabin. He told the court he did not awaken the captain (to warn him, when he and Ehlert crept into his berth) because he had not expected Ehlert to murder him, that Ehlert struck the moment he held up the lantern. He had not said anything as Ehlert had said he would kill him.

Eichstadt, the cook, was called to give evidence. He confirmed he was to be on watch from 2 until 4 that night, but was not called (one can imagine his disappointment). At 4 a.m. he heard the mate call out 'Fred (Muller), set the captain ashore' (loud enough for others to hear, no doubt). He did not see Muller until six o'clock that morning, and during the evening he smelled spirits on Muller's breath. The following day he searched Muller's berth and found the three bottles of spirits, 'not quite full', and the box containing the money of which he took possession. He recalled seeing the six 5-francs pieces at the captain's desk. Eichstadt asked Ehlert where Muller would get money and spirits. Ehlert said nothing, but later asked Eichstatd for the money, saying he would put it into the captain's cabin. Eichstadt refused to give it to him, saying he would wait until the captain returned.

Johann Wiedeman, the first apprentice, confirmed his watch was 4 till 6 on the fateful night, and that he saw Muller on deck when he ought to have been asleep, and Ehlert emerge from his cabin (hardly usual at that time). Wiedeman went to the captain's cabin to 'take away slops', and Ehlert told him to wash the floor. Ehlert explained – and Wiedeman would have expected an explanation at that time of night – that the captain had rang his bell and told him that he wished to go ashore. Wiedeman also said that he overheard Ehlert saying Muller had taken the money (the conversation between Ehlert and Eichstadt) – possibly spoken loud enough for his benefit.

Captain Berkholdz's body was found on a sandbank on the Thursday morning. He was identified by his clothing and a ring he wore. The heavy stone was still attached by the line to his body. Police superintendent William Brown told the court he and Inspector Bailes went aboard *Phoenix* at 8.30 p.m. on Thursday evening where they saw the mate, Jacob Ehlert. They had no interpreter. You might imagine the situation: two Sunderland policemen and a German-speaking crew …

They all went to the captain's berth. The bed was made, and the sheets were clean. But when the superintendent turned down a pillow he discovered a large bloodstain. Ehlert tried to leave the cabin and was arrested. Bloodstains were found on the front of his clothing, consistent with a bleeding nose. Supt Brown examined the cabin again the following morning, finding it had been recently washed and was still damp. The wooden bulk-head was produced in court, showing blood

A report into the murder of Captain Johan
Frederick Berkholdz.

on it, together with a piece of bloodstained flooring and a bloodstained
towel. Supt Brown said he 'examined the ship minutely', finding
smears and streaks of blood. On part of the window was a splinter with
a piece of red wool, corresponding with the shirt worn by Ehlert, and
there was blood on the frame of the skylight.

Insp Bailes told the court he saw the master of the steamboat, *Tiger*,
aboard the vessel, and received from him a bag containing a blue pea
jacket, a pair of grey trousers (which had come off in the water), some
foreign coins and other items, all identified as the property of the
captain, and a bag containing a bloodstained sheet. Muller identified
the jacket and the lantern, found by Insp Bailes in the mate's berth.
The master said that on Thursday morning *Tiger* was alongside a
foreign ship whose name he could not recall (*Phoenix*). A foreign man

had given him a bag containing property, which he subsequently handed to Insp Bailes. Mr Blech (the interpreter) said Ehlert, had made a voluntary statement, saying he was the man who handed the property to someone on *Tiger*.

So there we have it. The captain murdered by Ehlert, the motive theft with Muller made to stay silent at the time of the deed against pain of death, given stolen goods to encourage him, then forced to tell the crew he had taken the captain ashore after which his failure to reappear would lead people to believe he had vanished, and his cabin was nice and clean which proved nothing untoward had occurred there. One wonders if anyone in that courtroom thought for a moment that it might have been Ehlert, not Muller, who had told the truth, in the exact same circumstances, except that Muller, not Ehlert, was the murderer.

Only two persons were present when Captain Berkholdz was murdered – Ehlert and Muller. Thus, any evidence given by one could not be corroborated by anyone else. In the coroner's court, when Muller's evidence was read out, Ehlert denied everything Muller said, saying he knew nothing of the murder at all, that the blood on his shirt was from a nosebleed. He said he had seen 'the boy' (Muller) at the stairhead of the cabin, but had concealed this information out of compassion (implying Muller was the murderer). Ehlert demanded Muller be brought forward, so that he could confront him. This was done, whereupon each accused the other.

With no independent testimony, there could be no conclusive evidence against either man. Furthermore, it is possible they acted together in the murder of Captain Berkholdz; if so, a conviction was unlikely without corroborative evidence. To speculate: one turning 'Queen's Evidence' against the other would at least result in one conviction, so they chose Muller to give evidence against Ehlert. They might just as well have chosen Ehlert to give evidence against Muller! There were bloodstains on Ehlert's clothing, but that doesn't mean he wielded the fatal blows; both men were in the cabin, both would be bloodstained. Ehlert handed over the captain's belongings to the crew of *Tiger*. So what?

The jury heard the uncorroborated testimony of Muller. They believed him. Ehlert was the man the police said it was, so it must have been. Ehlert could not give evidence. In those days, evidence of accused persons was not permitted, as it was considered they were bound to say anything in their own defence. It took eight minutes to find him guilty. Ehlert maintained his innocence until the day they hanged him. Later, he gave this account of events on the fateful night.

'I was awoke at an early hour by a noise in the ship. I jumped up from my berth and saw the boy (Muller) rushing from the cabin steps. He exclaimed, 'I am betrayed', and ran towards the side of the vessel, apparently with the intention to throw himself overboard. I enquired what was the matter, when he said, 'Oh save me, I have killed the captain'. 'I observed, 'Let me satisfy myself that the captain is dead and

I will see what can be done'. I went down to the cabin and found the captain dead on the floor. The captain was no friend of mine, and I could now be of no service to him. I determined to befriend the boy and assisted him in the disposal of the body.'

Ehlert's brother, Carl, wrote a letter to the Prussian Vice Consul, pointing out that his 'unhappy brother may be innocent', and asked him to consider, if intending to murder the captain in the dead of night, he would have invited Muller along with a lantern to witness the event. As well as questioning motive, Carl Ehlert suggested putting Muller's account to the test. 'If a death sentenced were pronounced against Muller, perhaps the truth would come out.' In other words, sentence both and see what happens. No less just than believing one against the other.

As they prepared to hang Jacob Ehlert, he was asked, 'Do you willingly give up your life for the life you have taken violently?' Ehlert replied, 'I have taken no life at all.' These were the days before the measured drop, and the poor man struggled as he slowly choked to death at the end of the rope. A crowd of 3,000 turned up to watch. Before he was hanged, Ehlert's gaoler drew his attention to Luke, Chapter 12, verse 4: 'Be not afraid of them that kill the body, and after that have no more than they can do'. How reassuring for a man who might or might not have been guilty. Muller, of course, went free.

The hanging of Jacob Frederich Ehlert.

Point to Ponder

When someone turns 'Queen's' or 'King's Evidence', it is usually because they themselves are threatened with conviction, so they seek to 'help the police' in order lessen the charge against them, or at least lighten the sentence. Accomplices fall into this category of dubious witness. Their concern is their own welfare rather than the course of justice, and their testimony must be heard with care and corroborated by other facts. A court may or may not accept testimony from such persons. If there is evidence aplenty, it will not be needed. When evidence is in short supply, and an accused is likely to walk free, the evidence of an accomplice can be vital.

It must be evidence of the party who played the lesser part in a crime. A getaway driver at a bank robbery could perhaps testify that so-and-so robbed the bank and shot the cashier in the hope of favourable treatment by the court; the robber in such circumstances could hardly testify against the getaway driver in the same hope. In the Ehlert case, Muller gave 'Queen's Evidence' and Ehlert was convicted. Why not the other way around? Did the police, desperate to secure a conviction, care one way or the other?

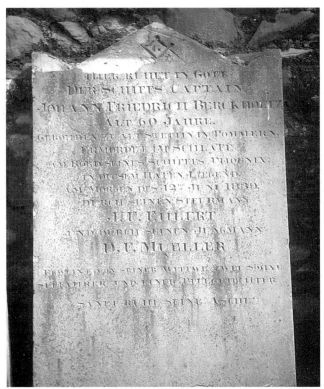

The gravestone of Captain Berkholdz in St Peter's Church, Sunderland.

Thomas Fury: The Man Who Wanted To Hang

Thomas Fury hated prison. And he'd had plenty of experience of it, serving at least thirteen years behind bars, not a good way to spend one's life, especially in Victorian Britain. So when, under the name Charles Henry Cort, he was sentenced to 15 years for robbery at the Old Bailey, he decided to confess to a murder he committed ten years previously in Sunderland. Enough was enough: Fury would rather be dead.

Fury was a sailor aboard the schooner, *Lollard*, which docked at Sunderland in February, 1869. Not unusually, he and a shipmate, John Lawrence, decided to hit the town for a night of booze and women. They drank their fill of the former, and Fury went on alone in search of the latter. He found it in the shape of an Irish prostitute, Maria Fitzsimmons, whose services included sexual gratification, but she stole Fury's money, for which she paid with her life. Fury stabbed her ten times, pushed her bloodied body under the bed and when *Lollard* later docked in the Thames he disappeared.

One month later, as one Joseph Dyson went for his morning dip in the Serpentine, Hyde Park, he found a black book in the water. Inside were some newspaper cuttings about the Sunderland murder,

Sunderland, *circa* 1860.

and a pencilled note amounting to a confession by 'the guilty man', whoever he was, details which could only have been written by the murderer. The notebook was handed to the police. Ten years passed. The Sunderland murder was a dead duck, left 'on file', as they say. Except that Fury, alias Cort, decided to resurrect it by confessing, in the knowledge that he would hang – which is precisely what he wanted. The prison governor was astonished. 'Are you in your right mind?' he asked. 'I'm quite in my right mind,' said Fury. Yet when he appeared at Durham Assizes he pleaded 'not guilty'!

Whether Fury regretted his actions, or had gone loopy due to spending years locked up is unknown. But having placed himself in the dock, the prosecution were more than happy to provide the evidence: first, the testimony of his former shipmate, John Lawrence, who confirmed he and Fury had gone on the town that fateful night, when Fury had had bought a knife, and who identified the notebook found in the Serpentine as his and which had gone missing from his locker aboard *Lollard*; second, handwriting evidence of an 'expert', who said the confession in the notebook was written by Fury's hand; third, the captain of *Lollard*, who identified Fury as his former crewman; and fourth, Fury's own, detailed admission.

Then, the worst possible scenario. Fury's barrister suggested that even if he had killed Fitzsimmons, he would be guilty of manslaughter, not murder, as he had acted in defence of his property. That would mean prison for life! Fortunately – or unfortunately, depending on whatever Fury's state of mind was by this time – the jury found him guilty of murder. He was hanged on 16th May, 1882, at Durham. Whether Fury was satisfied with the outcome is not known.

SECTION THIRTEEN

HANGING –
IS THERE A CASE?

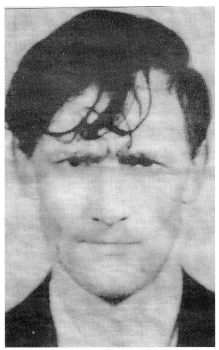

Gwynne Owen Evans (above)
and Peter Allen were hanged on
13th August, 1964, for murder
and robbery – the last lawful
executions in the U.K.

Capital punishment was abolished in this country over thirty-five years ago. There seems no doubt that the British public, if asked, would wish it restored. But has its abolition led to an increase in murders being committed?

This is a difficult question to address, not least because the answer lies with statistics. This shouldn't be too difficult, you might think; after all, there can't be that many murders. Unfortunately, statistics are manipulated to suit politicians' needs; statistics which start as 'murder' are liable to end up as 'manslaughter' by the time police, lawyers and the courts have done with them; statistics are cold figures, matched against real events which happen to real people.

Most murders, as highlighted in these pages, are perpetrated by people who are drunk, deranged, provoked, insane or temporarily not in control of their senses. Hanging them is no deterrent to other like-minded souls. Most murders are unplanned acts by people who didn't

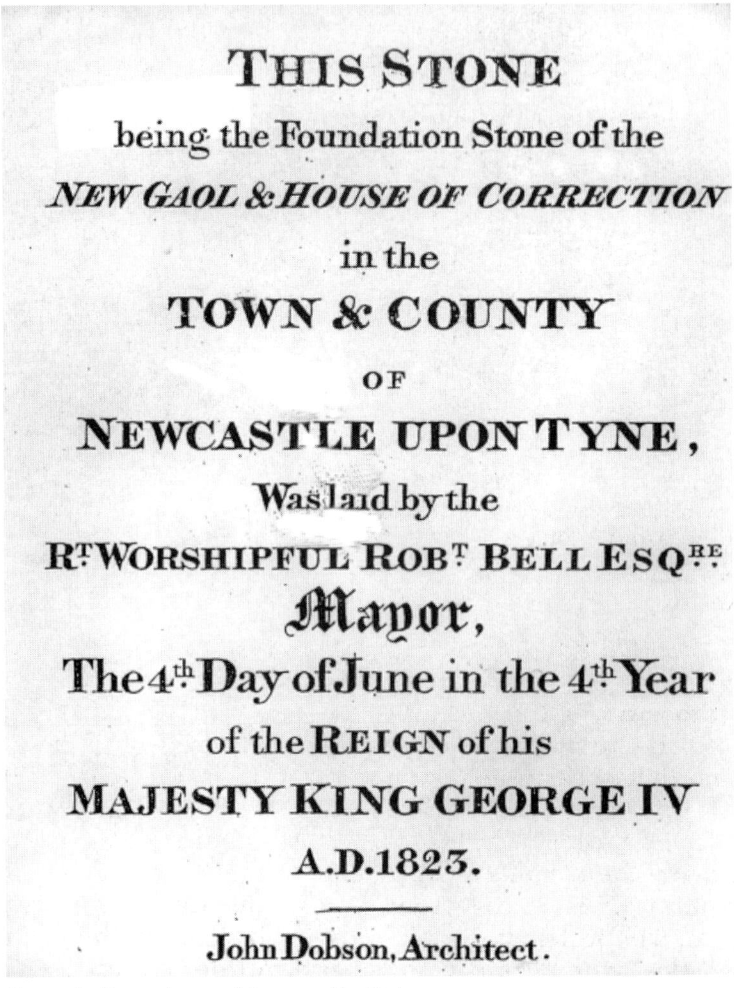

THIS STONE

being the Foundation Stone of the

NEW GAOL & HOUSE OF CORRECTION

in the

TOWN & COUNTY

OF

NEWCASTLE UPON TYNE,

Was laid by the

Rt WORSHIPFUL ROBT BELL ESQRE

Mayor,

The 4th Day of June in the 4th Year

of the REIGN of his

MAJESTY KING GEORGE IV

A.D.1823.

———

John Dobson, Architect.

Foundation stone, Newcastle Prison.

Inside Newcastle Prison, *circa* 1928. Have conditions improved today?

get out of bed that day intending to kill anybody. Others are committed in so-called 'cold blood' – the bank robber who shoots to steal, the sex-attacker (those not falling into the 'deranged' category) who must kill his victim or be identified. Do they stop to think at the thought of the noose? There were countless murders, pre-1964 (the date of the last hanging in this country) that 'hanging' didn't prevent. Thomas Fury preferred to die rather than serve a prison sentence. Prison conditions were Victorian then, you might argue. But are they much better today?

Even if hanging is no deterrent, you might think it's a deserving punishment. The killer of the old lady for her purse, the serial rapist. Or paedophiles, who sexually abuse and murder children. Would hanging them be justice? Maybe it would. Unfortunately, the problem in an imperfect world with an imperfect legal system is that there will be cases where the guilt of an accused is never truly established. String them up? Aye, but what if they are innocent? Stringing the wrong person up is a murder perpetrated by the state in your name; another statistic, and not one you might care for. You cannot put right a wrongful conviction once that trapdoor is released. What's more, the police will close the case as the real culprit goes unpunished.

A major problem in the criminal justice game, such as it is, lies with the fact that the players are human beings, and therefore have human failings. We have seen over-zealous police fashion evidence to suit their pre-judged opinions about who is 'guilty' of committing a crime. There can be no condoning such conduct. Yet it's not easy for honest coppers – the overwhelming majority, let it be said – to solve crime with one hand tied behind their backs in today's world of prisoners' rights, rules and regulations, and securing evidence against the clock under the Police and Criminal Evidence Act (which ensures that the right of an accused to remain silent preserves his civil liberty, but does nothing to further the course of justice). Working against time never improved anyone's standard of work.

Any breach of procedure by investigating detectives, however trivial, is picked up by defence lawyers and evidence thus gleaned is liable to be thrown out at trial, even though accurate and honestly gathered. Just one mistake, one step from the letter of the law and the whole case might be a dead duck. And there will be mistakes when honest coppers must look over their shoulders in anticipation of the stinging hand of criticism by the public, the media and even their own chief constables and senior officers, many of whom these days have little operational experience in today's world of fast-track promotion and political correctness. It is no wonder that police do their best to out-manoeuvre those who would seek to thwart their honest endeavours to prosecute a suspect to conviction. That doesn't mean they are always right. Such a system is liable to find the guilty innocent, reducing the chances of wrongful conviction. So it does. But it is just as likely to find the innocent guilty, and this is not acceptable.

There are many more stumbling blocks in the so-called criminal justice system. Witnesses may bear false testimony or simply be mistaken on some vital issue. There are technical points of law and countless other issues, manna from heaven to the Rumpoles of the Baileys of this world but which do nothing to serve the cause of justice. Even those who admit to a crime may not be telling the truth. The entire process is shaky, unreliable, downright dodgy. And we would hang people in its name?

Even without securing conclusive evidence a man or woman may yet be convicted: there remains the lurking danger of a mistake. Never mind today's advanced technology, mistakes there will be, and one is too many. Is it right to hang someone in these circumstances? Before you answer, put yourself, or a member of your family, in the place of someone wrongly accused – and then decide.

Acknowledgements

The author wishes to thank staff at Northumberland County Archives, Newcastle-upon-Tyne Central Library and Sunderland City Library, as well as at other libraries throughout the area, too many to mention, whose staff assisted in the research required in producing this book. Also special thanks to fellow writers Nick Cook and lifelong friend and former colleague and now fellow writer, Arthur McKenzie, for their valuable help, advice and encouragement in all my writing.

The Author

Paul Heslop served in two police forces, Newcastle upon Tyne City Police (later, after amalgamations, Northumberland Constabulary and Northumbria Police) and Hertfordshire Constabulary. He joined the then Newcastle City force in 1965, being posted to 'on the beat' duties in the City Central Division. These were the days of foot patrol, 'Tardis'-like police boxes and on-the-street supervision by sergeants and inspectors, days now, sadly, all but gone.

Over 30 years, Paul went on to serve in C.I.D., Special Branch (Ports) and Regional Crime Squads in both forces. As detective, he was involved in many investigations into murders and serious crimes, from

The author, Newcastle City Police. 'My mother insisted on taking this photograph. As you can see I wasn't best pleased'.

Tyneside to London and the South East. As detective inspector at Watford, Hertfordshire, his focus continued on serious crime: murders and suspicious deaths, rape and sexual offences, child abuse and domestic violence, both in investigative and training roles, as well as the day-to-day investigation of burglary and other offences.

Paul retired from the force in 1995, since when he has established a successful writing career: in 2000 he wrote his autobiography, *The Job – 30 Years A Cop*, and the following year *The Walking Detective*, an account of a walk he completed, alone, from Cornwall to Caithness. He now writes articles on health and safety, local history and walking, as well as a 'murder series' for two regional newspapers. He is an ardent 'fell walker' and a regular visitor to Scotland's 'Munros' (mountains over 3,000 feet). He now lives in the Lake District, where he runs a successful writing class, 'Writing for Publication and Profit'.

The author.

By the same author:

The Job – 30 Years a Cop

The Walking Detective

BY THE SAME AUTHOR

Ordering Details

The Job – 30 Years A Cop   ISBN: 0 9538066 0 X
£6.99 (£8.50 including postage and packaging)

The Walking Detective   ISBN: 0 9538066 1 8
£8.99 (£10.50 including postage and packaging)

Froswick Press, PO Box 7, Keswick, Cumbria, CA12 5GD

www.froswick.co.uk

THE PEOPLE'S HISTORY

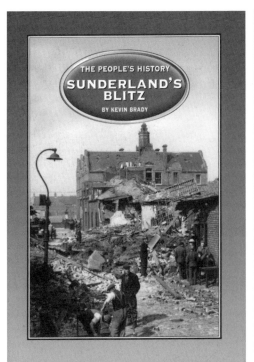

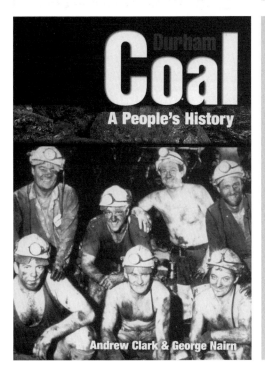

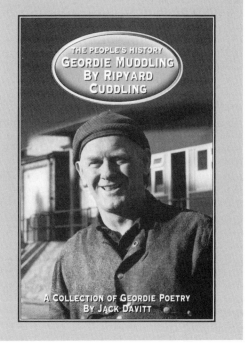

'If you give me six lines written by the most honest man,
I will find something in them to hang him.'

Armand Richelieu (1585-1642)
French Statesman and Cardinal

The People's History

To receive a catalogue of our latest titles send a large SAE to:

The People's History
Suite 1
Byron House
Seaham Grange Business Park
Seaham
County Durham
SR7 0PY

www.thepeopleshistory.co.uk